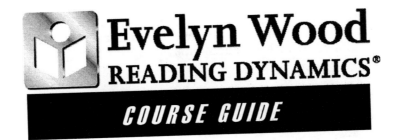

Copyright © 2007 Evelyn Wood Reading Dynamics
Overland Park, KS

Acknowledgements

Page from *The Book of Names* is reprinted by permission of the Southern New England Telephone Company.

"Reality of the People's Republic," a selection from *The People's Republic of China* by Claude Buss, is reprinted by permission of the Southern New England Telephone Company.

"The Myth of the Overworked Executive," a selection from *The Folklore of Management* by Clarence B. Randall, is reprinted by permission of Little, Brown & Company in association with the Atlantic Monthly Press.

"W-A-T-E-R," a selection from *The Story of Helen Keller* by Lorena A. Hickock, is reprinted by permission of Grosset & Dunlap, Inc.

"Height Requirement for Police Officers May Be Eliminated" and "Lincoln Center Adds Dancing to Cultural Life" are reprinted by permission of the New York Times Company.

Some passages have been edited for length and content.

Many years ago, while I was teaching in Utah, I began to work with the ideas of increasing the reading speed of my students. I knew there must be a faster, more satisfactory way of reading. I had read in history books about many fast readers.

Over a period of seven or eight years, I found fifty-three men and women living today who could read faster than 1,500 words per minute. The fast readers I discovered were represented in all walks of life. They were not necessarily geniuses. I tested them and found that they read with amazing speed and comprehension. None of the people tested had received training in reading, but they all enjoyed reading, read extensively, and read difficult materials at high speeds. These fifty-three exceptional readers, I found, had several reading characteristics in common: (1) they all read in a generally downward direction rather than left to right, (2) they absorbed the meaning of whole areas of a page at a time, and (3) they adjusted their speed to the type of material they were reading. After carefully observing and testing fast readers to see what they did that was different, I was able to develop, over a period of years, a technique that enabled me to teach myself to read very rapidly. This convinced me that these unusual reading skills could be taught and were within the reach of every normal reader.

Over a period of years I developed techniques and drills that were successful in dramatically raising the reading speed and comprehension of my students. To increase their speed, I taught my students to use their hand as a pacer, to keep their eyes moving generally down the page and to absorb patterns of words, rather than reading each word individually.

My educational background was enriched as the reading program developed. Over the years I received extensive academic training in reading skills, a Master's degree from the University of Utah, and broad experience in reading instruction at junior high school, senior high school, college, and adult education levels.

Today, classes are taught from coast to coast in major cities. To date, hundreds of thousands of people have been trained to read at these rapid rates. Students who have learned to read through Reading Dynamics include the Queen of Denmark, Mrs. Indira Ghandi of India, senators and members of Congress, state superintendents of public instruction, lawyers and law students, doctors and medical students, college professors, blue-collar and white-collar workers, housewives, retired people, and many reading teachers—over 300 of whom went through out extensive training program to become Reading Dynamics instructors.

These and other interested people who would agree with Dr. Robert Maynard Hutchins, former President of the University of Chicago, who said: "We do not need to burn all the books to destroy out western civilization. All we need to do is leave them unread for one generation."

Evelyn N. Wood, Founder

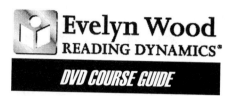

Approaching Dynamic Reading

Memory and Recall Strategies

Applying the Multiple Reading Process

Appendices

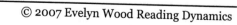

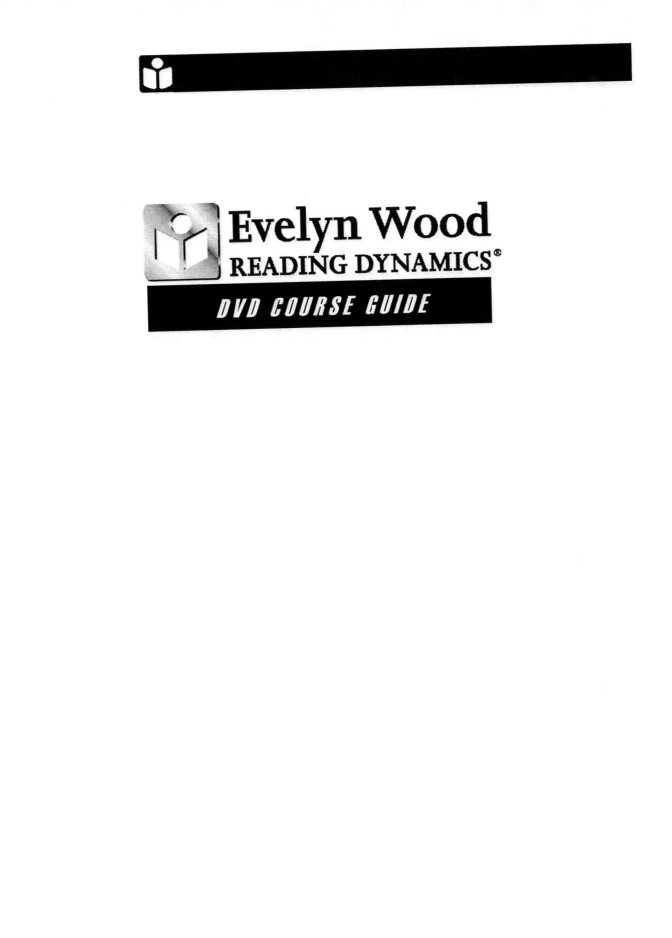

Evelyn Wood
READING DYNAMICS®
DVD COURSE GUIDE

Personal Improvement Log

	Pre-Test	1	2	Post-Test
Total # of words read	719			
Divide by # of minutes	3			
Total words per minute	239.66			
Comprehension score	83			

Calculating Comprehension Scores

Number of Questions Responsible for Answering

Number of Questions Correct		1	2	3	4	5	6	7	8	9	10
	1	100	50	33	25	20	16	14	13	11	10
	2		100	67	50	40	33	29	25	22	20
	3			100	75	60	50	43	38	33	30
	4				100	80	67	57	50	44	40
	5					100	83	72	63	56	50
	6						100	86	75	67	60
	7							100	88	78	70
	8								100	89	80
	9									100	90
	10										100

Personal Goals

What would I like to be able to do after this program that I am currently not accomplishing?	Specific Dynamic Reading/Dynamic Thinking techniques I can use to achieve these goals.
• read faster 7 3500 wpm • 95% comprehension w/very technical information • • •	• • • • •

Reading: A New Perspective

Reading Is...

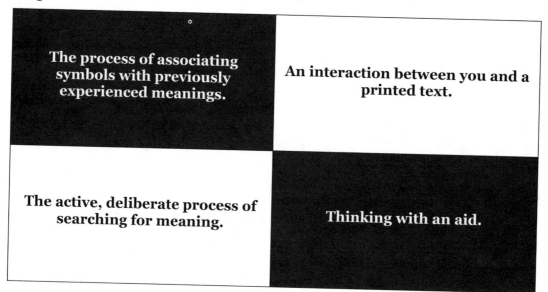

The process of associating symbols with previously experienced meanings.	**An interaction between you and a printed text.**
The active, deliberate process of searching for meaning.	**Thinking with an aid.**

Linear-Subvocal Reading Is ...

The process of saying words to ourselves

while reading one word at a time

from left to right.

Traditional Subvocal

SEE IT → **SPEAK IT** → **HEAR IT** → **KNOW IT**

Dynamic Visual

SEE IT → **KNOW IT**

Eliminating the Challenges of Traditional Reading

Fixations-25%

Regressions-15%

Recalcitrant Recovery-35%

Dynamic Reading Goals

- Smooth, efficient eye movement
- Full comprehension while reading
- More effective, focused mind

Purposes

- Eyes moving
- Mind responding

Benefits

- Curbs regressions
- Enhances perceptual ability
- Directs concentration
- Controls reading rate
- Promotes flexibility

Drilling vs. Reading

DEFINITION

Drilling: using visual, motor, and procedural skills to condition dynamic readers to achieve higher speeds and more thorough comprehension.

Characteristics of Reading Speed and Comprehension During a Drill

- 2-4x faster than comfortable comprehension
- Language and format
- Dialogue and description
- Always able to get something

Characteristics When Reading Instead of Drilling

- Only read as fast as YOU CAN UNDERSTAND!

Seamless Reading: Tips for Efficient Page Turning

Easy Handling: Breaking in a Book

1. Hold the closed book on a firm surface, flat on its binding

2. Open the front and back covers, pressing along the seam to keep them laying flat

3. Take a few pages at a time from the front and back and lay them next to the covers, running your hand along the seam to press the pages flat. Continue to the middle of the book.

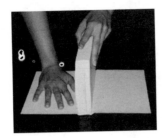 

Turning the Pages

Right-Handed

Pacing with the right hand

Turning with the left hand

Left-Handed

Pacing with the left hand

Turning with the right hand

Evelyn Wood Reading Dynamics

DEFINITION

Comprehension: Understanding what you read as you read it

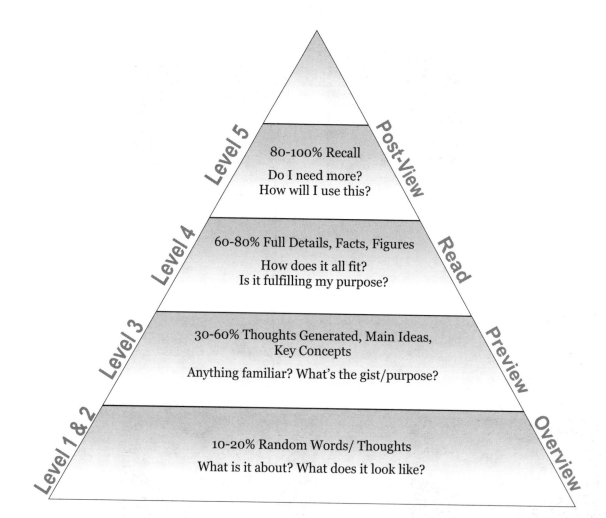

Level 5 — Post-View
80-100% Recall

Do I need more?
How will I use this?

Level 4 — Read
60-80% Full Details, Facts, Figures

How does it all fit?
Is it fulfilling my purpose?

Level 3 — Preview
30-60% Thoughts Generated, Main Ideas,
Key Concepts

Anything familiar? What's the gist/purpose?

Level 1 & 2 — Overview
10-20% Random Words/ Thoughts

What is it about? What does it look like?

"Reading furnishes the mind only with the materials of knowledge; it is the thinking that makes what we read ours."

- John Locke

The Question Mark Hand Motion

Purpose: To identify the structure of a document and overview its contents

Pace: 2-3 seconds per page

Time: 30 seconds to 2 minute maximum

Benefits:

- Softens mind to material
- Aids in determining purpose
- Allows a survey of the document
- Lets you initially prioritize
- Able to estimate total time needed to meet purpose

Your eyes should only **generally follow** the hand's movement on the page.

The "S" Hand Motion

Purpose: To identify the structure of, preview or read material, depending on your purpose

Pace: Varied to purpose

Time:

Overview	Levels 1-2	30 sec. to 1 min.
Preview	Level 3	2 to 4 min.
Read	Level 4	As needed

Benefits: Flexible to all levels of comprehension

Overview	Preview	Read

Dynamic Thinking:
The Fundamental Mind Activities for Recalling Information

Comprehension:

    Occurs during reading

Recall:

    What is left after reading is finished

Level 5 Thinking

Fundamental Mind Activities

SOAR

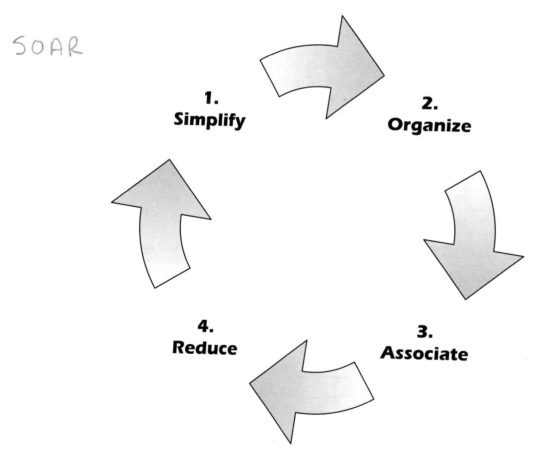

1. Simplify

2. Organize

3. Associate

4. Reduce

DEFINITION

Recall Patterns: Written material patterned logically and specially intended to represent the content, not reproduce it.

The Purpose

To record key information that will trigger the memory

Key Characteristics of Recall Patterns

- Related to reading, but developed separately

- Using your own words to represent what you understood

- Requires mental organization

- A reinforcement activity for comprehension

Goldilocks

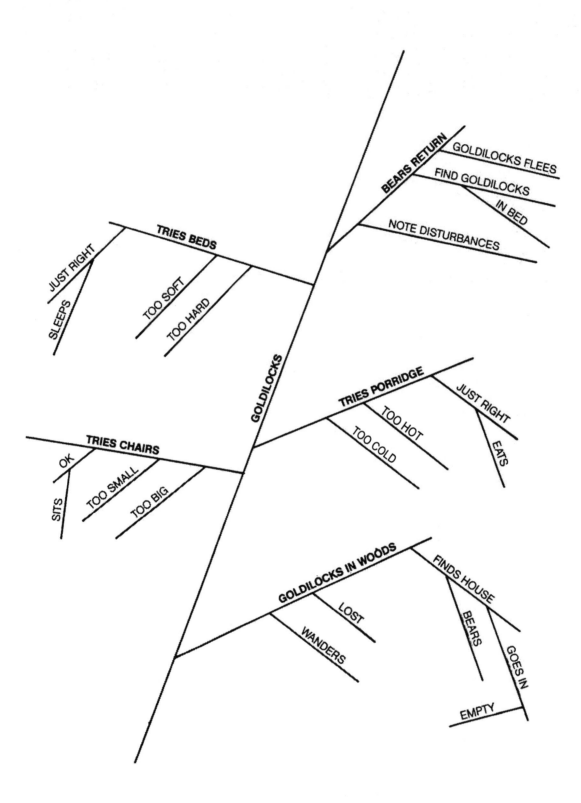

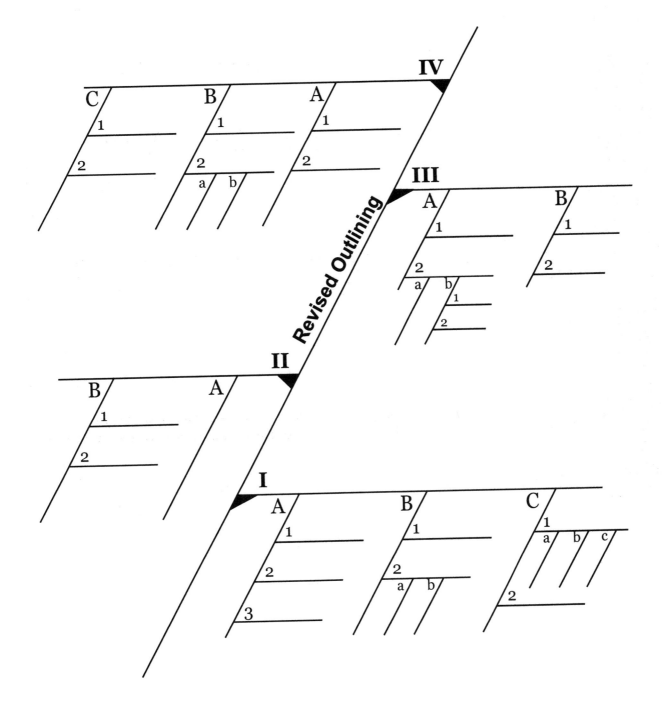

Revised Outlining

Putting It All Together

Pre-Reading	*General Overview*	Looking over features and structure of material
	Preview	Quickly looking through a document to identify the concepts, categories, and new ideas related to purpose
Reading	**Actual Reading**	Filling in the details of the information gathered during pre-reading
Post-Reading	*Postview*	Reviewing material to reinforce and discover additional information registered, but not learned, during actual reading

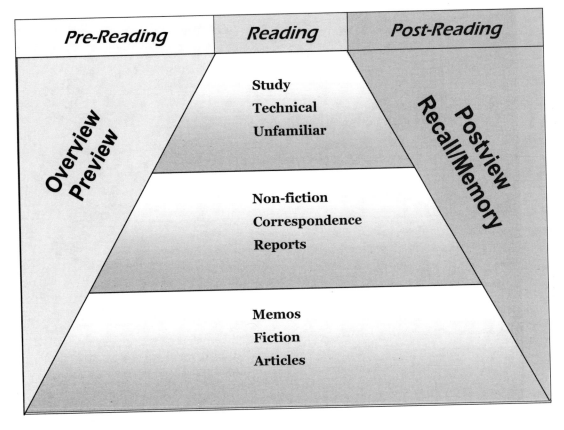

Pre-Reading	Reading	Post-Reading
Overview Preview	Study Technical Unfamiliar	Postview Recall/Memory
	Non-fiction Correspondence Reports	
	Memos Fiction Articles	

----------------------------Amount of time spent in 3 reading activities----------------------------

Hour
after
hour
I
kept
the
gun
pointed
at
the
other
nine
men.
From
the
lifeboat's
stern,
where
I'd
sat
most
of
the
twenty
days
of
our
drifting,
I
could
keep
them
all
covered.
If
I
had
to
shoot
at
such
close
quarters,
I
wouldn't
miss.
They
realized
that.
Nobody
jumped
at
me,
but
in
the
way
all
glared,
I
could
see
how
they
had
come
to
hate
my
guts.
Especially
Barrett,
who'd
been
Bos'n's
mate;
Barrett
said
in
his
harsh,
cracked
voice,
"You're
half
asleep
now!"
I
didn't
answer.
He
was
right.
How
long
can
a
man
stay
awake?
I
hadn't
shut
my
eyes
in
maybe
seventy
two
hours.
Very
Soon
now
I'd
doze
off,
and
the
instant
that
happened
they'd
pounce
on the
little
water
that
was
left.
The
last
canteen
lay
under
my legs.
There
wasn't
much
in it
after
twenty days.
Maybe a
pint. Enough
to give
each of us
a few drops.
Yet I
could see
in their
bloodshot eyes
that they'd

gladly kill
me for
those few
drops. As
a man
I didn't
count any
more. I
was no
longer third
officer of
the wrecked
Montala. It
was just
a gun
that kept
them away
from the
water they
craved. And
with their
cheeks sunken,
they were
half crazy.
The way
I judged
it, we
must be
some two
hundred miles
east of
Ascension.
The storms
were over the
Atlantic
swells, long
and easy,
and the

morning sun
was hot—
so hot
it scorched
your skin.
My own
tongue was
thick enough
to clog
my throat.
I'd have
given the
rest of
my life
for a
single
gulp
of water,
but I
was the
man with
the gun—
the only
authority in
the boat—
and I knew
this: Once
the water
was gone,
we'd have
nothing to
look forward
to but death.
As long as
we could
look forward
to a drink
later, there

was something
to live for.
We had to
make it last
as long as
possible. If
I'd given in
to the curses
and growls, if
I hadn't
brandished the
gun, we'd
have emptied
the last
canteen days
ago. By now
we'd all be
dead. The men
weren't pulling
on the oars.
They'd stopped
that long ago,
too weak to
go on. The
nine of them
facing me were
a pack of
bearded, ragged,
half-naked
animals, and I
probably looked
as the rest.
Some sprawled
over the
gunwales
dozing.
The rest watched

as Barrett did,
ready to spring
the instant that
I relaxed. When
they weren't
looking at my
face they looked
at the canteen
under my legs.
Jeff Barrett was
the nearest one.
A constant
threat.
The Bos'n's
mate was a
heavy man, bald,
with a scarred
and brutal face.
He'd been in a
hundred fights,
and they'd
left their marks
on him.
Barrett had been
able to sleep—
in fact, he'd
slept through
most of the
night—and I
envied him
that. His eyes
wouldn't close.
They kept watching
me, narrow and
dangerous. Every
now and then
he taunted me in
that hoarse, broken

voice: "Why don't
you quit? You
can't hold out!"
"Tonight," I said.
"We'll ration the
rest of the water
tonight." "By
tonight some
of us'll be dead!
We want it now!"
"Tonight," I said.
Couldn't he
understand that
if we waited
until night the
few drops wouldn't
be sweated out of
us so fast? Barrett
was beyond all
reasoning. His mind
had already cracked
with thirst. I saw
him begin to rise,
a calculating look
in his eyes. I
aimed the gun at
his chest and he
sat down again. I'd
grabbed my Luger
on instinct twenty
days ago just
before running for
the lifeboat. Nothing
else would have kept
Barrett and the rest
away from the water.
These fools, couldn't
they see I wanted a

drink as badly as
any of them? But,
I was in command
here—that was the
difference. I was the
man with the gun
who had to think.
Each of the others
could afford to
think only of
himself; I had
to think of
them all.
Barrett's eyes
kept watching
me, waiting. I
hated him. I
hated him all
the more because
he slept. He had
that advantage
now. He
wouldn't keel
over. And long
before noon I
knew I couldn't
fight any more.
My eyelids were
too heavy to
lift. As the boat
rose and fell
on the long
swells, I could
feel sleep
creeping over me
like paralysis.
It bent my head.

It filled my brain like a cloud. I was going, going... Barrett stood over me, and I couldn't even lift the gun. In a vague way I could guess what could happen. He'd grab the water first to take his gulp. By that time the others would be screaming and tearing at him, and he'd have to yield the canteen. Well, there was nothing more I could do about it. I whispered, "Take over Bos'n." Then I fell face down in the bottom of the boat. I was asleep before I stopped moving. When a hand shook my shoulder, I could hardly raise my head. Jeff Barrett's hoarse voice said, "Here, take your share of the water!" Somehow I propped myself up on my arms dizzy and weak, I looked at the

men, and I thought my eyes were going. Their figures were dim and shadowy but then I realized it wasn't because of my eyes. It was night. The sea was black; there were stars overhead. I'd slept the day away. So we were in our twenty-first night adrift—the night in which the tramp Groton finally picked us up. I turned my head to Barrett. There was no sign of any ship. He knelt beside me, holding out the canteen, his other hand with the gun steady on the men. I stared at the canteen as if it were a mirage. Hadn't they finished that pint of water this morning? When I looked up at Barrett's ugly face, it was grim. He must have guessed my

thoughts. "You said, 'Take over, Bos'n,' didn't you?" he growled. "I been holdin' off these apes all day." He lifted the Luger in his hand. "When you're boss-man," he added with a sheepish grin, "in command and responsible for the rest, you sure get to see things different, don't you?"

1.

2.

3.

4.

5.

6.

7.

8.

9.

10.

1. The officer in charge carried what kind of weapon?

2. The boat had been drifting for how many days?

3. The bos'n mate's name was ...

4. The officer in charge had been awake for how many hours?

5. What was the approximate location of the drifting boats?

6. What was the weather like?

7. How many men faced the officer in charge?

8. What did the men want so desperately?

9. Describe the appearance of the men in the boat.

10. When the officer keeled over, what did the bos'n's mate do?

Type of Material	Organization	Overview Techniques	Preview Techniques
News Articles Technical & Scientific Documents	"Inverted Pyramid" Abstract or Lead Conclusion or Summary Most important data to detail in descending order of importance	Overview headlines & subheads (breaks are usually arbitrary). Overview physical organization. Find sections, parts. See captions, charts, pictures, etc.	Read summary in first paragraphs (for news articles). Read summary, introduction, conclusion. Examine body for unusual features (graphs, questions, tables, etc.).
Magazines Journals	**Three ways an author can organize a magazine article:** *Chronologically* *Magic Formula* (eye-catching first paragraph, followed by the author's point of view, observations and details) *Train of Thought* (each paragraphs serves a different purpose)	"Don't put it off." Glance at table of contents. Mark "high impact" articles. Briefly prioritize marked articles. Look over entire magazine to notice bits of information missed in the TOC.	Read first and last paragraphs of marked articles in priority order. Look over body for unusual features.
Correspondence Memos	Opening and closing paragraphs are usually cordial formalities and contain little vital information. The earlier and later middle paragraphs contain the most critical information.	Who sent it? Expecting something? Who else received it? Date sent? Can I infer what it's about?	Focus attention on the middle paragraphs. Isolate the purpose of the letter/memo—does the writer want action, information, a response?
Non-Fiction Most Textbooks Newspaper Feature Stores & Editorials	Introduction of main ideas Body (sequential development of key ideas) Conclusion Key information tends to lie at the beginning and ending of sections. Pattern repeats within subsections.	Read dustcover. Check out table of contents, and index, for overall organization. Look over the physical organization. Locate subsections, how many parts, etc.	Read beginning and ending of main section. Look over whole for key ideas; find main ideas only. See beginning and ending of key subsections, looking for main ideas only.

Catch yourself skipping an overview.

Remember that overviewing material creates a framework into which information can be effectively organized, understood, and remembered.

Collect what you know, set a purpose, and prepare to compare.

Remember the importance of bringing relevant knowledge and experience to your reading. Ask "what do I already know about this material?" Set a purpose for your reading that will guide you to locate, organize, and assimilate new and valuable information.

Use pre-reading as an opportunity to challenge yourself.

As you pre-read at a fast pace, attempt to "stretch" your ability to see more words and quickly organize information in your mind.

Balance two needs:

a) Approaching reading with flexibility.

b) Continuing to develop all components of the Multiple Reading Process.

As you continue to practice all of the specific components of Dynamic Reading, remember that once you feel relatively comfortable with the process as a whole, a key to successfully applying it will be using only skills and approaches which fit your purpose.

Experiment with different hand motions.

Especially during your initial practice, continue to remain flexible in the ways you use your hand. You'll eventually develop a collection of motions from which you can select the most effective methods for your particular purpose.

Create while you read.

Approach each piece of reading material as a "springboard" for your mind. Consistently try to generate unique images and phrases in your mind, which represent most effectively for you what the author is saying.

Use recall patterns to support Dynamic Thinking.

Consistently try to organize what your mind creates as it reads.

Allow yourself to solidify and deepen comprehension—postview.

Allow yourself to selectively reread—and add to your recall—important material that warrants deeper analysis.

If you're reading to learn, strengthen your knowledge base.

Organize your recall patterns and specifically schedule brief segments when you can review and apply the information in them.

Whenever you can, put your newly learned information to use.

Teaching, explaining, or even just mentioning newly learned information helps to further solidify it into your mind.

Albert Einstein
By Arthur Beckhard

Chapter One

"CHASING THE 'X'"

"Why do I have to go to school, Papa?" Hermann Einstein, tall and severe looking, looked down at his ten-year old son. "Do you want to grow up to be an ignoramus, Albert?"

"What's an ignoramus?"

A burst of laughter came from a corner of the large, comfortably furnished room. Father and son turned quickly toward Mrs. Einstein, who was seated at the large black piano.

"Oh, Hermann," Mrs. Einstein exclaimed, her voice still bubbling with laughter, "you'll never beat Albert at that game!"

"I'm sure I don't know what you mean," her husband sputtered.   95

"There's no use in pretending," Mrs. Einstein replied, as she went on playing an old Hungarian folk song. "I heard you and your brother deciding that the only way to keep Albert from asking so many questions was to answer him by asking him a question. But you see, it didn't work. He can always outlast you!"

Albert crossed the room and stood beside his mother, for a moment forgetting what he had asked. Her fingers fascinated him. They were such stubby, soft little fingers, and yet they danced and fluttered across the keys with the speed of a robin running across the lawn. They hit the keys so firmly, without fumbling or hesitations, that they made the piano fairly sing. They leaped and pounced upon two final crashing chords. Mrs. Einstein swung herself around on the piano bench and took Albert into her arms.   240

She looked over the top of his dark, curly head and smiled up at her husband. "You see, there is a way to make Albert stop asking questions. My music will do it."

Mr. Einstein nodded, smiling. Before he had a chance to answer, Albert wriggled around in his mother's arms so that he could turn and face her.

"Is it wrong to ask questions?" he asked.

Now it was Mr. Einstein's turn to laugh.

"There he goes again!" He chuckled. "Even your music can't stop him for long."

Mrs. Einstein looked at her husband reprovingly, and she gave Albert a small hug.   343

"There's nothing wrong in asking questions," she said fondly, "as long as you don't do it just to tease or embarrass people or to make them seem foolish."

"I don't do it like that," the boy protested. "I do it because there is so much I don't know—so much I want to know. I want to know all about everything right away."

Albert's mother smiled proudly, but his father drew his heavy eyebrows together. He looked puzzled.   421

"If you really mean that, Albert, how is it that you could ask why you must go to school? School is the place where questions should be answered."

"But they're not!" Albert cried out. "They don't even let anybody ask questions, and they'd never think of answering them. I hate school! It's like being in prison. The teachers are like prison guards marching up and down between the rows of desks."   492

Mr. Einstein and his lovely wife exchanged a look that was full of meaning. What could they say in answer to their son's charges?

The Einsteins had moved from the little city of Ulm, in Bavaria, in 1880, a year after Albert was born. Mr. Einstein and his brother Jacob, who had foreseen what would happen to Bavaria, had packed up and brought the whole family to Munich. There the two brothers set up a small chemist's shop. They had been there only a year when Albert's little sister, Maja, was born, and the family moved into a large comfortable house just outside the center of town.

599

It was not long before "the Einstein House," as people called it, became one of the most popular places in the whole city of Munich. Often when permanent residents had guests from out of town they took them to the Einstein house for an evening of conversation and music or poetry reading. These evenings were so much discussed that often visitors to Munich would, upon arrival, ask their hosts if they could possibly arrange for an invitation to the Einstein's.

679

An invitation, however, was scarcely necessary. There was nothing formal about these affairs. Sometimes Mrs. Einstein would play Mozart or Brahms compositions. Sometimes she would sing folk ballads of Germany and Austria. On some evenings, the guests all gathered around the piano and sang old songs they all knew. Both Mr. Einstein and his brother had deep, pleasant voices and could lead their guests in these familiar melodies.

747

Many times neighbors and friends gathered just to talk in the warm, friendly living room with its deep maroon wallpaper lighted by the orange glow from the gaslight chandelier that hung from the white ceiling, and the evening sped by without allowing time for any music at all. Young Albert hated to go to bed on these occasions. He listened, wide-eyed, to the talk of new inventions like the electric light and the telephone. His father and Uncle Jacob were well posted on all the latest scientific developments, particularly those which might affect the sale of equipment and the electrochemical apparatus. Their shop was far ahead of their competitors in all such matters.

860

There were times when Albert's father would decide to read aloud from the works of great German writers such as Goethe, Schiller, and Heinrich Heine. Young Albert could never decide which kind of evening at home he liked best. Certainly there was a great contrast between learning in the friendly atmosphere of his own home and the austere school classrooms where the pupils were punished for failure but never given praise or encouragement for accomplishments.

935

Mr. and Mrs. Einstein spent a good deal of thought in the selection of a school for Albert. He had been backward as a small child, slow to learn to talk and read, and very shy. They had selected a Catholic school considered the very best in Munich. They were dismayed when the government took over the operation of all the schools and began installing military rules and regulations.

1004

"The true culture of Germany is being submerged by militarism," Mr. Einstein exclaimed sadly.

But neither of Albert's parents had realized the extent to which the Prussian army had taken over the public school system until Albert's very real unhappiness became apparent to them.

"They make us memorize the day's lesson," the boy told them. "They don't tell us what it says or what it means, but we must learn every single word. And I can't. Unless I know what a thing means, I just can't remember it. And so they open the drawer and take out the ruler..."

1103

His mother hugged him and kissed the palm of his hand, still red from the strokes of the steel ruler. She looked up at her husband appealingly. Mr. Einstein shook his head.

"There's nothing we can do," he said. "They will question our loyalty if we complain to the principal." He sat down and beckoned Albert to come closer.

1162

"Albert," he said, placing a friendly hand on his son's shoulder, "your mother and I don't like this any more than you do, but we must all face it. You are old enough now to understand what is going on in the world around you. The army is becoming more and more important in Germany and in Austria. It will not be long before the army rules the country. Even now, army officers are buying up big businesses. So far they have bought only the larger stores. But soon they will see that Mr. So-and-So has a nice little candy store on the corner. They will buy the store across the street. Then they will tell everyone that they must stop buying candy from Mr. So-and-So and must, instead, buy from the new store. That is the way it usually works out when the military becomes too important." 1310

"The real reason why you must go to school is that there is a law in Germany that no one may get a job unless he has a diploma. You will have to finish six more years of primary school and high school before you can get one; and some day you may have to get a job and help me and Uncle Jacob support your mother and little Maja."

Albert looked into his father's face and saw that he was not fooling. The situation was serious.

"I won't complain anymore, Father," he said. "I'll try my best to get along in school." 1413

Then he turned and, with his head lowered, eyes staring at the flower pattern in the carpet, he started toward the door. In the doorway he turned.

"Perhaps I could earn money playing my violin," he said. "Then I wouldn't have to have a diploma."

"I'm afraid you would have to practice a long time to learn to play well considering the possibility in all seriousness."

"Wouldn't mind practicing if I knew why," Albert explained. "And I don't mind it anymore—" 1495

"Albert," his father interrupted, "I don't think it would be a good idea. It's never a good idea to do something you love doing just for money. It always spoils it."

"What's that? What's that I hear?" A big voice shouted from the little foyer just outside the living room. It was Uncle Jacob.

"Hermann, did I hear you telling the boy that it was wrong to get money for doing a job you enjoy? That's poppycock and you know it!" 1576

Uncle Jacob was a big man, much taller and heavier than Albert's father; his booming voice always seemed to carry a great deal of authority. Now he turned to Albert and addressed him with all the seriousness of a defense attorney pleading his client's case before a judge and jury.

"My boy, try to understand what I'm saying. You should always try to do work you love. And if you find yourself in a spot where you have to do work that you dislike, you must find a way of making yourself like it so that you can do it well." 1677

Albert looked doubtful. He shook his head. "I hate school," he said stubbornly.

"Albert!" Mr. Einstein said severely. "I don't want you to use that word. There is enough hate in the world without hating such a thing as schoolwork."

He lapsed into silence as Mrs. Einstein put a quieting hand on his arm. Uncle Jacob crossed over to the fireplace and lifted his long porcelain bowl pipe off the mantel. 1748

"I think I can show you what I mean, boy," he said. "What subject do you hate most?"

Albert thought for a moment before answering.

"I can't decide between algebra and geometry. I hate — I mean I dislike them both."

Uncle Jacob grinned. 1791

"There's no reason to hate or dislike either of them. They're both the laziest kind of mathematics. Look, I want you to try something, an experiment."

He paused for a moment and Albert waited. "Do you ever play policemen, or pirates, or anything like that?" Uncle Jacob asked.

"Sure."

1840

"Well, try playing detective for a change. You're looking for a villain. You don't know whether he's a thief or a pickpocket. You don't even know his name. All you're sure of is that he's somewhere around and you've got to find him to keep him from doing any harm. First thing you do is give him a name for your files. Right?"

Albert nodded, his eyes glistening with excitement. "You call him 'X'."

Again Albert nodded.

1917

"Then you tail him. You follow him into one formula and out of it and into another or you slide down the hypotenuse of a triangle after him and chase him up the side wall of a parallelogram. Finally you catch up with him. You find out what he is and who he is. Now you've got him! You put the cuffs on him and take him in. That's all algebra is. Or geometry. Like to give it a try?"

"Yes." Albert said earnestly, "I would. I think that would help a lot."

2010

1. **Mrs. Einstein was seated:** (67 words)
   a. at an electric organ.
   b. on a round piano stool.
   c. at a large black piano.
   d. at a small well-tuned piano.

2. **Mrs. Einstein had the long tapering fingers of an artist.** (241 words)
      T   (F)

3. **Albert's curiosity was** (468 words)
   a. satisfied by the demands of school.
   b. unsatisfied because teachers didn't let anyone ask questions.
   c. limited to science.
   d. challenged by the game he played with his father.

4. **The Einsteins had moved from the city of _____ in Bavaria in 1880.** (531 words)

5. **Albert's sister was named:** (600 words)
   a. Marie.
   b. Marta.
   c. Maja.
   d. Mara.

6. **The Einstein house was:** (679 words)
   a. where Mrs. Einstein played her own compositions.
   b. so popular that it was necessary to have an invitation to go there.
   c. a friendly place with its blue living room and its subdued lighting.
   d. one of the most popular places in the city of Munich.

7. **The Einstein brothers sold electro-chemical apparatus in their shop.** (863 words)
      T   F

8. **Albert as a small child, had been:** (1008 words)
   a. backward, slow to read and learn.
   b. average.
   c. outgoing and friendly.
   d. happy in the friendly atmosphere of school.

9. **Albert, as a child, attended a Catholic school in _____.** (1008 words)

10. **The Prussian Army:** (1052 words)
   a. was criticized by the Einsteins because of their school methods.
   b. had very little effect on the schools.
   c. took over all the schools.
   d. took over the public but not the parochial schools.

Hand Motions, Speed, Comprehension

15-Minute Rewards Keep You On Track

When completing a task, we feel a sense of accomplishment. However, if just completing the task were reward enough, we'd finish everything we set out to do. Many of us, however, are procrastinators. Simply completing a job isn't always a sufficient incentive. A good way to end procrastination is to boost the rewards we receive when we finish a job, says time management expert Lucy H. Hedrick.

Consider these examples she offers of people who work hard, are considered successes, but don't feel satisfied. Peter, in his twenties, is a foreman for a construction company. He makes a good salary, working a 60-hour week. Peter likes his work, but complains he has too much to do. He falls into bed at night, often too tired to eat, only to start all over again the next day. 145

Sarah, a computer programmer and single parent of two young boys, begins her day at 6 a.m. She eats lunch at her desk so she can complete her work by 5 o'clock. After feeding, bathing and reading to the boys at night, she sorts mail, starts laundry and retires, exhausted.

Donald, 52, is president of an international bank. He seldom sees his family. His days are an endless series of meetings. He often thinks of getting out of the rat race, but never has time to give the idea much thought. 236

Each of these people has important tasks to do that he or she puts off. Peter is terrified his truck will break down on his busiest day, but he can't seem to get it to the shop. Sarah needs to clean her sons' closets and buy new winter clothes, but doesn't get around to it. Donald wants to sell his vacation home, which simply sits unused, costing him property taxes, but he puts off calling real estate brokers.

Hedrick says we are accustomed to giving rewards to others but not to ourselves. Employees at Donald's bank receive bonuses, and Sarah's children receive allowances for doing their chores. Similarly, we must learn to give ourselves "bonuses" so we will move ahead and do what we need to do. 363

Hedrick suggests planning "15 minute rewards" for completing unappealing tasks. Make a list of things you can do in 15 minutes that would serve as work incentives for yourself.

Peter, the foreman, came up with these rewards: have a cup of coffee, walk around the block, stop at a park and lie under a tree, and browse in a hardware store. Sarah would like to: browse in a bookstore across the street from her office, call a friend and chat, and have a cup of tea away from her desk. Donald said he fantasized: calling up one of his children just to chat, holding all calls and meditating for 15 minutes, or reading a spy thriller. 479

Try to reward yourself immediately after you complete an unappealing task. Also, reward yourself appropriately. When you adjourn a long meeting, take a walk around the block. When you finish the first draft of a five-year marketing plan, have lunch with a friend. If punishment should fit the crime, the reward should fit the accomplishment. List the tasks you tend to procrastinate and the bonus you'll give yourself when you actually take care of them.

554

Sleep Studies Put Your Mind at Rest

Why is it that when you get too much sleep, you feel more tired than when you went to bed? Some sleep-laboratory studies show that less sleep can translate into deeper sleep. "Short sleepers" (6 ½ hours) and "very short sleepers" (5 ½ hours) get as much or more deep sleep than "long sleepers" who average 7 ½ more hours a night; and deep sleep is what makes you feel refreshed in the morning.

635

Why? It's simple, says the Mayo Clinic's Dr. Peter Hauri. If your body needs only seven hours of sleep, but you habitually stay in bed nine hours, your body will begin to "spread" the amount of sleep it needs over that extra two hours – much as water released from a reservoir spreads out over the land. Since shallow sleep is less restorative, you awake sluggish.

781

The slumber of "short sleepers" is less disturbed and more efficient. They fall asleep more quickly, sleep more soundly and wake less often during the night, studies show. Besides reducing the amount you sleep, you can improve your sleep in other ways.

823

Don't climb into bed until you're ready to sleep. Sleep specialists have found that insomniacs virtually "camp out" in bed – they read, watch TV or lie awake thinking. They don't see bed as a place to sleep, but a place to do things. If you can't fall asleep in 20 minutes, don't fight it – get up, go to another room and engage in another activity. Don't go back to bed until you're sleepy. If you usually lie awake at night fore more than 20 minutes, cut back your sleep by 30 minutes. This can help you reach your optimum amount of sleep. Many people who think they're insomniacs are merely naturally short sleepers. Usually, people need less sleep than they think.

895

944

Get on a regular schedule. You can't keep a room temperature constant if you're always fiddling with the thermostat. Similarly, your body has a "sleepostat" that kicks in an hour or two before your established bedtime. Your temperature starts to drop and your system slows, including brain waves. Your body is signaling the brain that bedtime is approaching.

1002

If you do go to bed at 11 p.m. during the week and then stay up until 1 a.m. on weekends, you body gets the message that you're retraining it for a later bedtime. Then when you try to return to your regular bedtime Sunday night, you won't be able to. Your body has adjusted to weekend rates and needs a day or two to switch back. When your sleepostat receives confused signals, it goes haywire. Your brain over-rules your physical impulses, telling the body not to

1089

relax, since it might suddenly be called on to go out and dance the night away. This is what happens with jet lag – your body still clings to its accustomed time standard, though your brain knows it's not yet bedtime in your present locale. So go to bed the same time each night. Stick to your new bedtime and wakeup time even on weekends. Not only will you establish a shorter sleep time, you'll sleep better and wake more refreshed.

1723

Prepare your surroundings. How often have you been drifting off, then remembered you forgot to shut a window or turn off the bathroom light? Even when we're exhausted, a disruption in falling asleep can keep us awake long afterward. Develop a checklist before you turn the covers. Will it be too cold by morning if you leave a window cracked? Is the toilet running? Is there a cover handy if you get cold?

1242

Get into a bedtime routine. Sleep specialists recommend that you prepare for bed as much as an hour beforehand to cue your body to relax. A glass of milk, a warm bath or a volume of Proust are all good for making you drowsy. Relaxation or biofeedback exercises relieve stress. People who practice these achieve brain activity similar to sleep's early phases.

1304

Finally, don't take your worries to bed. If you have a problem, common wisdom says to "sleep on it" – mull it over just before bed and in the morning a solution may pop into your head. But this just disturbs sleep and causes nightmares. Nighttime worry habits cause so many sleep problems that some people even come to associate bedtime with worry. They go through a calm day and then, when they lie down at night, trot out all their concerns to count over, like sheep jumping a fence.

Put the sheep out to pasture, click out the light, and make the most of your sleep time.

1411

Shift the Focus from Mistakes to Possibilities

Our society conditions children through reward and punishment: They are "good" if they make an "A"; "bad" if they make an "F." Consequently, they see correction not as constructive but as a threat to their self-esteem. It's tough to change people's behavior when they fear looking bad, says author Victor Elliott. Their customary approach is "reality" to them. New approaches seem "crazy" and therefore frightening.

929

It's like the technique animal trainers use to train a young elephant. They shackle him to a short, heavy chain attached to stakes driven in the ground. The beast soon "learns its place." When full grown, the elephant can easily pull up the stake. But, by then an ankle cuff, attached to nothing, serves to limit its motion. It believes it's tied down and can't run away, so it doesn't.

999

We too have mental maps of "how things are." Our conditioning creates many maps which now don't reflect reality. Yet we rarely question our maps' accuracy, unless some input provokes a fresh reaction. People resist "changing their minds," but they're often willing to shift their attention to something different: A new perspective often helps break up an old mental habit.

1059

For instance, a 12-year-old girl swimmer was losing races, even though she was an excellent swimmer. Her coach, Joan, asked, "Do you want to win?"

"Yes," the girl said.

"Why do you think you can't?" Joan asked.

The girl answered, "I can't get enough air."

"So if you could get enough air," Joan responded, "you could win?"

The girl nodded her head.

Joan told her, "When you swim, count how many breaths you take on each lap."

1136

The girl changed the focus of her thoughts and easily won the next race. Elliott believes a shift of attention, from what we focus on now to what we usually ignore, can break us out of our conditioned response. For example, had a client who always ran behind schedule, upsetting himself, his own clients and his staff. Elliott suggested he keep track of everything that happens when he saw clients on time for the next two days. Elliott refocused his view from this old pattern (being late) to the times he deviates from it (the instance he's on time.) By the third day, the man was seeing 90% of his appointments on time.

1248

To demonstrate this mental shift to groups, Elliott asks for volunteers who view a ball being tossed at them as a threat. (It also helps if they think they're clumsy.) He tosses them the ball and watches as they awkwardly attempt to catch it. After a few times, Elliott asks them to "notice the lines on the ball when it comes to you. Don't worry about catching it; just notice which way the lines are moving." Once they shift their focus, the old conditioning ("I drop balls thrown to me") is set aside, and they easily catch the ball.

1347

One elderly woman, who quickly went from being scared to catching the ball with one hand, at first had described herself as "clumsy." Elliott asked her when she had decided that. When she was six, she said, her brothers wouldn't let her play ball with them, calling her "clumsy." That experience formed her self-image, which prevailed for more than 60 years.

When things become a challenge, not a threat, the mind and body relax. Refocusing people's attention increases their awareness.

1427

Women's Approaching to Leading

When women achieve high positions in management, do they perform their jobs just like men do? In many aspects, the answer is no, says journalist Sally Helgesen. Rather, women's management styles differ from those of their male counterparts.

1469

To compare men and women managers, Helgesen referred to a now classic study by Henry Mintzberg, who kept a minute-by-minute record of the work activities of five male executives. Helgesen studied closely four women executives, comparing their work patterns with Mintzberg's men. She found several distinctions.

Work pace. The male managers worked at an unrelenting pace, permitting no breaks in activity. In a day jammed with scheduling meetings and unexpected encounters, they seldom paused.

1543

The women worked at a steady pace but scheduled small breaks throughout the day. They used pacing tactics to cut back on stress, such as closing the office door during lunch, reading on the sofa, and scheduling 15-minute intervals between meetings. One woman manager described this pacing as "a recognition that I'm only human and I need my peace of mind."

1604

Interruptions. The men's days were characterized by interruption and fragmentation. They spent lots of time "putting out fires" and felt besieged by both significant and trivial events. They used their secretaries to "shield" them from their subordinates, whom they viewed as "usurping" their time.

1648

The women, however, were concerned with keeping the relationships within their organization in good repair. If subordinates needed their attention, the women saw the interruptions as part of their work, rather than an interruption of it. The women also used their secretaries as conduits to help them communicate with the world – not as shields to protect them from the world.

1708

Outside activities. The male managers spared little time for activities not directly related to their work. They severely curtailed the time they spent with their families, often viewing their homes as "branch offices." They made little time for pursuing outside interests and confined their reading almost entirely to job-related literature. They were intellectually isolated, with a deep but narrow focus.

1768

The women managers, however, made time for non-work related activities. None were willing to sacrifice their families, which they viewed as a priority. They geared their work arrival and departure times to mesh with the needs of their children, and they discouraged their employees from working on weekends because "they have families, too." None of the women were as intellectually focused as the men. They read history, psychology, mysteries, novels and tabloids – anything to keep them in tune with current trends in the world. As well, they made time for collecting art and pursuing other hobbies that both broadened and relaxed them.

1870

Time for reflection. Immersed in the day-to-day need to keep the company going, the male managers had little time for thoughtful planning and contemplation. Their hectic pace kept them focused on short-term matters.

1903

The women, on the other hand, kept the long term constantly in focus. They described a need to make a difference, not just to their companies but to the world. To that end, they allowed time for solitude, reading, and keeping abreast of world events that might have a bearing on their work.

Job identification. The men identified strongly with their jobs – so strongly that they couldn't detach from them to play a variety of roles (figurehead, team builder, liaison).

1983

Although the women took their jobs seriously, they viewed their jobs as just one element of who they were. Other aspects of their lives, such as raising children, took up too much time to permit total identification with their careers. As a result, they could detach from their position to play any part called for. One woman manager kept two offices. In the first, she assumed the role of "people manager" and focused on accessibility. In the second, she played corporate chief.

2065

Information sharing. Sitting at the top of the pyramid, the men had easy access to information. But they tended to hoard it as a source of power and were reluctant to share it. This often caused organizational bottlenecks and was a prime cause of cumbersome workloads.

The women viewed themselves as being in the center of things, rater than at the top. So they found it natural to reach out and share information. The women shared information in innovative ways such as inviting employees to sit in while they gave phone interviews.

2157

Overall, the language the male managers used to describe their work tended to be negative. They spoke of interruptions, usurpation, protection, burdens, and shield. These words reflect managers who feel pressured by the demand of their work, have a strong sense of their own importance, and view others in their organizations as means to an end.

The women, on the other hand, described their work life with words such as flow, interaction, reaching, network, and involvement. Their language reflects managers who emphasize relationships with people, focus on doing tasks rather than completing them, and see both work and people as ends, not means.

2260

Successful Self-Marketing

By Russell Riendeau

Let's listen in on these two one-sided telephone conversations:

"Hello...Oh, yes, that young man, Mr. Presley? Yes, I'll speak with him...Good morning. Elvis, is it? Oh sorry, Elvis. Well, Elvis, I've had a chance to listen to that demo tape you made for our company, and I just don't think that sound is going to be popular. Sorry, we won't be considering you for our record label. But thanks anyway, and good luck."   78

"Universal Studios, good morning! Well...Ronald Regan. How are you? The last picture you made was great. What can I do for you? ...Oh, you want to run an idea by me? What are agents for? Go ahead, shoot...I see. You want out of motion pictures ...Politics? ...Do I think you could be governor of California? I guess so. And if you get enough votes, you could be president of the United States! Hey, wouldn't that be something? Well, let me know what happens. Keep in touch."   164

I'm not sure how historically accurate those conversations are. However, the point is clear: Marketing yourself to an indifferent world is possible and mandatory for success. My goal is to give you some strategies for getting through the doors you need to get through and for being heard.   212

Let's assume that you've chosen a goal, a field of interest, a career path, or a company that you want to join, and you have a burning desire to make it happen. OK, now what do you do? Ready-set-wait, and wait, and wait, and nothing happens. Why? Well, you've heard of the law of physics that says, basically, a body in motion tends to stay in motion. The reverse of that law is true as well. Nothing will happen if you don't start something. And how do you get started? How do you engineer a propulsion system to shoot you toward your destination? Let's find out right now.   320

When you decide to take on an important task, goal or mission, you begin to attract ideas and get hunches that eventually lead to new feelings and experiences. These will prepare you for the upcoming events. This is due to another law of physics: like attracts like. By learning how to market yourself with more direction, you'll be in the right place at the right time more often and, therefore, get more interviews, job offers and opportunities than seemed possible to you before. If Elvis Presley and other performers could overcome initial rejection and go on to become superstar entertainers, and actor Ronald Reagan could ignore ridicule and go on to become president of the United States, doesn't it make sense that your goals have a good chance of becoming reality?   451

Let's look at four key points in the examples of Elvis Presley and Ronald Reagan.

First, each of them had a goal. Their goals were big enough to attract plenty of doubters, yet to raise the eyebrows of a few who saw them as special individuals who had a purpose, who believed in themselves and who had the courage to develop and use their talents and follow their dreams.

520

Second, they worked at it. Overnight success is rarely overnight. It takes months and years of preparation, with time invested in direct proportion to the benefit received. Having it all doesn't mean having it all now. Patience, persistence and planning pay pure profit.

563

Next, they had goals that would make a difference in people's lives. Their goals would have an impact on others. You see, if your dominant goal is so personal that only you benefit, you're not able to attract and use the energies of the universal powers to create change. This doesn't mean that a personal goal isn't worthwhile or is selfish. That's not the point. We all have personal goals, too, and they're important and help us to become better adjusted, more content, healthier and more pleasant persons.

651

Finally, they both stared with the talents they already had. You have tremendous talents and potentials within you that have yet to be developed. The most exciting opportunities lie within reach and are within sight of you right now. Look closely, and then look again.

696

If you haven't identified a worthy goal to pursue, one that is of your own choosing, or if you need a little guidance, I encourage you to do as I have done – and still do for that matter. Listen to many of the fine motivational audiocassette programs that have been released. This is an excellent way to build your self-esteem and, at the same time, gain ideas that will help you to identify a goal or definite aim in your life.

777

You must also market yourself to become "user-friendly." By highlighting your experiences, talents and employment history colorfully and in detail, and with all the feelings that you possess, you'll be seen in a favorable light. Prospective employers will be able to visualize you in the role you desire.

825

For example, if you wish to obtain a sales position and you don't have sales experience in the industry – or any sales experience at all – you should stress the talents you already possess. Stress your involvement in civic organizations, social groups and community events, especially positions to which you were elected and in which you were respected. Demonstrate your power to persuade. Find a way to link your experience to the prospective employer's frame of reference.

901

We were all raised to play it safe and reduce risks in our lives. This was to protect us, obviously because we were loved. And while playing it safe is important to your personal and financial well-being, it's not the mind-set to have when you're looking for a challenging career direction. And you need to understand that even though you're willing to take the risk, the person you're interviewing with – or whoever has the power to grant you the job – is remembering the same risk-aversion mindset he was taught, and he sees you as a risk to him if you don't work out in the job. Now what?

1009

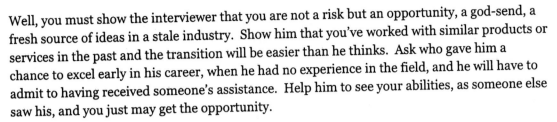

Well, you must show the interviewer that you are not a risk but an opportunity, a god-send, a fresh source of ideas in a stale industry. Show him that you've worked with similar products or services in the past and the transition will be easier than he thinks. Ask who gave him a chance to excel early in his career, when he had no experience in the field, and he will have to admit to having received someone's assistance. Help him to see your abilities, as someone else saw his, and you just may get the opportunity.   1106

Having spent the past 16 years in management and the professional-recruiting marketplace, I've seen hundreds of individuals go on to excel in industries far removed from their previous line of work or hands-on experience.

Following are tips for marketing yourself in the best light possible. I've seen them work time and time again to help people land their desired position or pursue their calling in life.   1173

Look closely at your current position in life or business. There may be tremendous veins of gold right under your feet, and yet you're not looking down. If you've been in your industry for a length of time, you're probably an expert in it by now and aren't giving yourself the credit you deserve. Maybe you can sell that expertise at a premium as a private consultant to current customers or to similar industries. Or, if you make your talents known through self-marketing and attract the top people in your field, you could even start your own company. Ask yourself, "Is the reason I'm looking to make a change really the market's fault, or do I need to adjust my thinking and use all the talents I have?" Wisdom doesn't come from how much you know; it comes by realizing how much you don't know.   1318

Just as location, location, location is the key consideration when buying real estate, research, research, research is the crucial element when setting sail into uncharted waters. Talk with successful people currently in the business. Ask them why they stay; and ask those who got out of the business why they did so. There could be some pitfalls not seen upon initial examination. Look carefully at the types of personalities in that market. Do you fit in, and would you want to?   1399

Remember the importance of preparation. Once you've secured an interview or meeting, the show is on. Everything you do and say will be graded by the persons you meet. Have a game plan. Anticipate the concerns they'll have with your background, and have solid, well-thought-out answers ready. Learn as much as possible about the people you'll be meeting. Talk with competitors, former employees – anyone you can – to get insight into what makes the industry thrive or stagnate and what the top performers do to be successful.   1485

Well, here's some new information for you to digest. When a person is trying to make a transition into a new field, the number-one knockout factor early on in the interview is inappropriate appearance. If you look like you belong, you can get in almost anywhere (you've probably heard that already, too). This doesn't mean looking pretty or handsome. It means wearing a style of clothing and hair suitable for the industry. It means clean fingernails,   1561 polished shoes, a nice pen in your pocket, a neat, error-free resume and solid documentation of past success in previous jobs. Those all are textbook practices, but they are often regarded as frivolous items that will be glossed over when prospective employers see how great you are. No way.

Look the part. You're probably saying, "Old news. I've heard it all a thousand times already."   1626

Be honest with yourself. If you're 34 years old and have a lifelong dream to play center for the Chicago Blackhawks hockey team, that's a fantasy, not a realistic goal. However, you can experience the same excitement level by playing in leagues, coaching, going to games, participating in adult fantasy camps for hockey enthusiasts. There are lots of ways to get the enjoyment while still remaining in a more traditional line of work that matches your abilities. One of my mentors always told me, "Work with the talents you already have, and be the best in those areas first. Then get some more." God gives us all equal talents – just in many different areas. Enjoy and use yours today.   1745

Finally, have courage. You'll encounter some strong criticism along the way to your dreams. Human beings often act in accordance with their fear of loss, which is often stronger than their desire for gain. But if you feel stronger about what you want to gain, about what you feel is right for you and will benefit you, your family and society, and then work toward it with all the tenacity and enthusiasm you can muster, you'll become what you've set out to be.   1828

This next decade will see unprecedented increases in service-related industries. Keep your dreams firmly in mind, and get started today on marketing yourself to an indifferent world. It's waiting for you to take the ball and run with it.   1867

Albert Einstein
By Arthur Beckhard

Chapter Four

"UNEMPLOYED SCIENTISTS"

The Swiss Federal Polytechnic Institute came as a revelation to the seventeen year-old boy. If Albert was a young man without a country, so were many of the others registered at the great university.

There were refugees from Czarist Russia. There were students who had been deprived of the right to get an education in Hungary, in conquered Bavaria, and some from Poland and even some from France. From every part of Europe, freedom-loving people of all ages had come to this sanctuary where they could develop their abilities in their chosen fields.

Aarau had seemed like the home of freedom. How much more inspiring to Albert was this great campus, with its hundreds of Swiss and foreign students all working side by side.

From the beginning of his university career, Albert was seized by a desire to become "a citizen of the world." Here, where individuals from practically every European country were gathered together, patriotism or nationalism seemed out of place and ridiculous. 95

Now, for the first time, he began to regret that he had not tried harder at the Gymnasium to master more languages. He longed to discuss their mutual problems with his fellow students, and yet could not talk or understand their language.

It did not take long for him to realize that mathematics had a language of its own, a language that was understood by people who could not understand each other. The symbols of algebra, geometry, calculus, physics, and chemistry were all that was needed to permit people of different languages to work out problems together.

It was this newly learned knowledge that brought about the crumbling of the wall he had always built between himself and strangers. He found that he was no longer shy with fellow students who, side by side with him, were seeking the basic truth of the universe. 239

During his four years at Swiss Federal Polytechnic, Albert made three very close friends. There was, first of all, Friedrich Adler, a blond boy who was even more bitter than Albert about the evils of militarism. He had seen his parents killed by a conquering German Army, and he believed that nothing good could come of conquering by force. Since Albert had seen the disastrous results military discipline had brought about in Germany's public schools, he was a willing listener and soon became a firm believer in Friedrich's pacifist theories. Both boys decided they would never join the army to right for any country, and they agreed that it seemed better to be shot as a traitor if their example could persuade others of the uselessness of trying to win arguments by force. 372

Marcel Grossman, who had been born in Switzerland, listened to Friedrich's impassioned arguments but disagreed with them. He believed that one should fight in defense of one's country. The other two boys conceded that Marcel had every right to his own beliefs and did not attempt to win him over. All three did their homework together and spent a great deal of their time in each other's company. 440

The fourth member of the group was a girl. Her name was Mileva Maritsch. From his very first meeting with her, at the table they shared in the physics lab, she fascinated Albert, because she was so completely unlike any girl he had ever met. She believed women should be educated. Most girls seemed to think that all they had to learn was how to cook and keep house for their future husband.

513

She spoke only Serbian of which Albert could understand not a word. And yet her eloquent eyes and long graceful hands enabled her to convey her meaning clearly in a sort of sign language of her own. Albert began studying Serbian, and Mileva got to work on unraveling the mysteries of German.

It was not long before she was able to explain to the three boys that she did not believe that girls should marry. The Emperor of Germany, Kaiser Wilhelm, had expressed the belief that women did not need to have an education or to know anything about politics or government. According to him women should concentrate on the three *K's-Keuche, Kirche* and *Kinder*, which in English would be the three C's – Cooking, Church and Children. Mileva could not say enough about her scorn for this belief. She felt that women should be free to accept jobs and to work side by side with men. She believed in the equality of women long before it was stylish to hold such ideas. She wanted to learn enough physics and chemistry so that she could go back to Serbia and teach the poor people who could not afford an education.

712

As soon as Albert explained her views to the others, the three boys, greatly relieved, welcomed her as a companion. Now that they knew she had no silly romantic ideas about love-making or marriage, they were glad to discuss their class work with her and seek her help in doing their homework.

All four members of this little group loved to take walks. They all liked music, and the beautiful old city of Zurich had much to offer them. Whenever their work schedule permitted, they enjoyed an evening of pleasure and relaxation.

804

Time sped by rapidly. Mr. Einstein sent money to Albert regularly. When Albert went home for this third summer vacation, he discovered why this had been possible. Karl Winteller had given the Einstein business the young blood and the drive it had lacked before. It was not making a fortune but there was enough money to support the whole family. Karl and Maja had waited for Albert to return and act as best man at their wedding, and he was overjoyed to see how happy the young couple were, and how well Karl fit into the family. His father seemed even less robust than when Albert had last seen him, but he insisted that he had never felt better in his life. Mrs. Einstein was so happy that she seemed to have grown younger instead of older.

941

Perhaps seeing his sister and Karl so happy had something to do with what happened when he returned to school. It was the last thing in the world he would have guessed. He fell in love with Mileva. Even more surprising, in spite of all her ideas on the subject, she fell in love with Albert. They became engaged and began to make plans at once.

1007

They agreed that they would be married just as soon after graduation as possible. They would both look for teaching jobs and with their fine record expected to get them easily. As soon as either one of them got a job they would be married. Mileva could only get work in a private school because she was a Serbian citizen but Albert had applied for citizenship four years before. By autumn following graduation the five-year residence requirement would have been fulfilled so he could get a position in any one of the government-controlled schools – even the Swiss Federal Polytechnic itself. Both Albert and Mileva worked harder than ever to improve their marks so that they could be graduated with high honors in physics, chemistry and mathematics in order to quality for the best jobs available.   1142

On graduation day, when they were handed their diplomas, Friedrich Adler and Albert Einstein were singled out for special mention. Albert was named the finest mathematician the university had ever graduated. But the next day when the four friends gathered in front of the bulletin board they soon learned that neither Albert not Friedrich, in spite of their honorable mention, nor either of the others had been given a job.   1212

They learned, too, that a vacancy on the faculty of the Swiss Federal Polytechnic had been filled by someone with a Swiss name. The four unemployed physicists turned and walked away in disconsolate silence. Three of them were angrier about Albert's situation than they were about their own.

"After all," Mileva said, breaking the long silence, "I am a woman. There had never been a woman professor in Switzerland. I can understand that they would hesitate. But Albert whom they called the greatest mathematician..."   1296

"It's a great disappointment, Albert," Friedrich said, "but try to cheer up. There will be something soon. I'm sure of it."

"The trustees know nothing about my pending citizenship," Albert said mildly. "They may not have wanted to give this plum of a job to a foreigner. It may be that they think I've not had enough teaching experience."   1355

"But you have!" Marcel exclaimed. "You're a great teacher. If it weren't for your tutoring I'd never have been able to get my diploma. And there are lots more like me."

"And have you told the faculty that, Marcel?" Albert asked. His eyes twinkled and he grinned at his angry friend. "Of course you didn't. And nobody else did either."   1415

Chapter Five

"SHOEMAKER'S JOB"

"But what will you two do now?" Friedrich asked Albert and Mileva as the four of them sat at a table in one of the many attractive little restaurants that were patronized largely by students. "You can't get married without a job and there's no telling..." "I'm going to stay right here, Friedrich," Albert said. "I think I'll be able to pick up some tutoring work for the summer school. Who knows, I may even be paid for it!"

1498

Marcel and Friedrich both laughed.

"Not you," Marcel chuckled. "If somebody tells you a hard-luck story or shows you a hole in his socks you'll hand him back his tutoring fee to have his socks mended."

"I've heard there's a job open in Winterthur. I'm going there to see if I can't grab it," Friedrich said.

"Isn't that supposed to be a pretty tough school? Almost like a reformatory?" Marcel exclaimed.

1569

"The tougher the better," Friedrich answered. "It'd give me a chance to test some of my ideas of teaching without resorting to beatings or any other forms of physical punishment."

Marcel turned to Mileva. "What about the fourth member of the quartet? Staying here with your beau?"

They all turned to look at her, and Albert gave her hand a squeeze. He fully expected her to say she would wait and see what luck he had in his job-hunting before making any plans. But she surprised him. She released her hand from his and spoke quickly.

1665

"I'm going back to Serbia," she said. "If Albert can't get a teaching job here, I certainly can't. In my country the standards are not quite as high as here. The need for teachers is greater. And besides, I speak the language better than either German or French."

"But, Mileva," Albert protested. "We promised each other we'd get married as soon as just one of us has a job."

1734

"Well? I am going to try. If I get one, we can get married."

All three of them stared at her in amazement.

"You mean you think Albert should come to Serbia to live?" Friedrich exclaimed incredulously. When she nodded he went on mercilessly, "You shouldn't even suggest such a thing. Albert is by far the most brilliant of us all. He has a great future. Would you want him to give it up and vegetate in some little far-off village?"

1815

"Who says he would vegetate?" Mileva answered, her eyes flashing angrily. "Don't you all talk all the time about science being above nations – more important than the world itself? Does it matter so much where Albert does his figuring, his endless experiments, his constant reading?"

"But Albert will get a position of importance here soon," Friedrich said. "He can have access to the best labs, the best equipment. It will have a certain amount of prestige..."

1891

"And you want me to forget about my own work and wait for him." Her eyes flashed. "Why should I! He's not willing to wait for me. Aren't you asking a lot?"

Albert looked at her. He had a strange premonition that marriage would not work out for two such ambitious people, but Mileva seemed very beautiful to him at that moment. Anger had brought color to her usually pale cheeks and her eyes seemed large and very moving. He reached out and took her hand again.

1978

"You must do what you feel is right," he said gently. "Go back if that's what you want to do. I'll stay here and try my best to get a job. Give me a year, Mileva. That's all I ask – give me a year to make good."

The others were embarrassed. Someone changed the subject, and that was the way the matter rested.

Two weeks later, when Albert had still been unable to find a teaching job, Friedrich came to him one evening.

2061

"Albert, you know I've been engaged for the next term at the technical school in Winterthur. It's not quite as bad as Marcel claims. It's not like a reform school, but the boys do all come from poor families who want them to learn a technical skill by which they can earn a living. They're not likely to be interested in abstract science. But what I thought was this. If it would keep Mileva here, you could take my job at Winterthur for one semester, just as a temporary thing until something better comes along for you."

2158

Albert was deeply moved. "Friedrich, I don't know what to say. No one has ever offered to do something so wonderful, but. . . I'll accept your offer, with all the gratitude in the world. Someday perhaps I'll be able to repay you. Do you think they will accept me as a substitute in Winterthur?"

"Accept you? When your credits are so much greater than mine? They'll jump at the chance."

2229

He was right. The authorities at the Winterthur Academy were delighted to have him as a substitute, and Mileva agreed not to return to Serbia but to wait at least until Albert had taught for one full semester in the little "reform school."

From the very first day, his teaching there proved to be a difficult assignment. Often it taxed his patience almost to the breaking point. The boys had a whole parade of new teachers. None had been able to maintain discipline. Albert got to the classroom a half hour before the class was scheduled to begin, and began writing a formula on the blackboard.

2335

At eight-thirty the boys came in like a flood released by a broken dam, yelling, singing as they rushed for their seats. Albert remained with his back to them, apparently unperturbed, as he continued to write on the blackboard. He waited a few moments for them to settle down, but the noise continued. The boys shouted at each other, shot spitballs from rubber bands, and threw wadded paper all around the room. After what seemed like endless waiting, Albert turned around and held up his hand for silence. To his amazement the young roughnecks quieted down momentarily.

2432

Albert stepped around the corner of the big desk and began.

"I am your new professor. My name is Einstein. I hope that we will..." That was as far as he got.

"Einstein, Einstein, good old Einstein!" Some of the boys began to chant in a rhythmic singsong. Others yelled other rude remarks.

2485

Albert knew it would be useless to ask again for silence. He had sense enough to know that they were trying to make him lose his temper and that the louder he talked the more noise they would make. Instead of trying, he turned to the blackboard and began to write:

Those of you who do not wish to study under me can go home. 2550

The boys gasped in amazement. Some of them started to their feet as if to leave the room, but others pulled them back into their seats. This was too good to be true. It was some kind of a trick. Those who left the room would probably be severely punished.

The noise faded. A few whispers were hushed. Albert turned from the blackboard to face them, and professor and pupils eyed each over warily like dogs who walk stiff-legged around each other before they decide whether they are enemies or friends. After a long moment, Albert, more than half expecting to be interrupted by whistles or catcalls, spoke quietly. 2659

"Your parents have doubtless paid good money for you to be in this classroom so that you may learn things that will help you master a trade."

He paused. The silence remained unbroken.

"I am going to stay here because that is what I am being paid to do. But I can't teach you if you don't want to learn. So I meant what is written there behind me on the blackboard. Those of you who wish to can go home. You will not be punished by me. If you can explain it to your parents' satisfaction you need never report here again." 2762

A minimum of whispers ran through the class but no one stood up. Knowing that a smile would serve to indicate to the boys that he was gloating over them, he remained solemn.

"There's one more thing," he said. "No matter what you do – anyone or all of you – you will not be punished by force. There will be no whippings, no slaps with a ruler. I don't believe in that. I stood too much of it when I was in school." 2844

There were no more whispers, just an attentive silence. After a moment he turned and, still with no smile or other sign of friendliness or what the boys would have called "softness," crossed to the blackboard.

"Today's lesson..." he began and proceeded to explain the formula he had previously written. 2894

That was his first great victory, and it gave him confidence. There were outbursts from time to time. There was occasional insolence, but nothing as extreme as that first day had seemed to promise. At the end of the semester, parents and faculty alike felt that he had accomplished a near miracle.

Whether they had really learned a great deal or not Albert was not sure, but he was certain of one thing. He had won the respect of his students. 2975

During his term at Winterthur, Albert had written to every university in Switzerland and France applying for a job as instructor or assistant professor. When the job ended and Friedrich Adler came to relieve him, he had received not even a nibble. Friedrich had done his best for Albert in Zurich, but he, too, had to report failure.

"You've done a wonderful job here," his friend argued stubbornly. "Something will come along. It must. What are you going to do next?" 3056

"Go back to Zurich, see Mileva, and try to persuade her to wait another six months."

"And if she refuses?"

"Then I will let her go to Serbia."

"Will you follow her if she succeeds in getting work?"

"Yes, I have promised." 3098

Friedrich looked as if he wanted to say something – possibly to urge Albert not to do anything foolish, not to throw away the chance of a brilliant career – but he changed his mind. He knew that it was not wise to try to interfere with two people who were in love.

Mileva met Albert at the railroad station. The long separation had made them both realize how much they meant to each other. As he took her in his arms Albert hoped that nothing would ever separate them again. He wanted marriage and a home. He must find a job at once to make this possible.

3204

Friedrich had reserved his old room in the boardinghouse for Albert. When he left Mileva and went there to leave his bags and books, he found a letter awaiting him. It was from Marcel. Marcel had something to talk to him about. It was important.

And so it proved to be.

"It's a job," Marcel said several hours later as they sat with steins of good beer on the table between them. "But I'm ashamed to mention it to you."

3284

"What do you mean, ashamed?" Albert asked. "What kind of a job is it that you hesitate to name it? I've told you I must find a job – any kind of job – at once. I want to get married."

"But this is just a shoemaker's job."

"But that's fine!"

Albert had often heard the expression. It had been a favorite of his father's. A "shoemaker's job" was a bread-and-butter job – one that had no prestige, brought no glory, but paid enough to cover living expenses.

"That's the very thing I want, Marcel. Tell me what it is."

3381

"Well – some members of my family are connected with the Swiss Government. I asked my uncle if he could help me find something for a friend of mine. I didn't tell him it was for Einstein who graduated from the university with top honors. I didn't want anyone to know that you haven't got the kind of position you should have..."

"*Please*, Marcel, out with it! Everybody pats me on the back and tells me I'm the greatest mathematician since Newton, if not actually Copernicus, but nobody will give me a job. Now you actually have one for me, and I can't get you to tell me what it is!"

3491

"It's in the patent office in Berne. It's checking inventions that people send in with their applications for patents. You have to see that there's no conflict – that no one else has patented the same idea already. That's all."

"It's wonderful! It's just what I've been hoping for. When can I start?"

3543

"Right away, just as soon as..."

"I'll be married a week from Saturday. Then Friedrich can come from Winterthur to be best man and still get back for classes on Monday. You will give the bride away. Marcel, you're wonderful."

"I hope we're not making a mistake," Marcel said.

"Don't be so gloomy," Albert told him. "Of course we're not making a mistake. Let's go tell Mileva."

3610

Goal #1

Chapter Six

WHAT IS RELATIVITY?

The job in the patent office proved to be everything that Albert had hoped it would be. Checking on inventions – some of them daring and obviously intended to make life easier for people, and some of them just crackpot ideas that could have no possible use – provided enough stimulus to hold his interest without making demands on his time after hours. He soon discovered that he could go back to thinking out the important problems that had tantalized him for so long. And he also learned that he gained a great deal by being able to discuss these projects with Mileva.

3716

She, too, was happy and anxious to provide the companionship her husband seemed to need. During the first few months of their marriage, Mileva quite often expressed the intention of getting a teaching job or position as a laboratory assistant. Before she actually got around to carrying out this idea, she learned that they were going to have a child. When their son, Hans Albert, was born, Mileva, in spite of her talk before marriage, became a careful and devoted mother. More than a year later, a second son, Edouard, was born to the Einsteins. Mileva found bringing up two healthy boys was a full-time job.

3822

Although he dearly loved his sons, Albert, at first, missed his wife's companionship. This loss proved to be a blessing in disguise for he turned more and more to the study of physics to fill in hours that would otherwise have been lonely.

More for his own amusement than with any serious purpose in mind, Albert began to write up some of the examples that seemed to disprove theories that had long been taken for granted. As he finished them, he submitted them to a publication called *Annalen der Physki*, or *Annals of Physics*. To his surprise, the first one was accepted by the editor, and it appeared in the following issue. Letters began to pour in to the publication from all over Europe. Some of these praised Albert as a man of vision and imagination. Most of them called him a radical and crackpot. From that time on, Einstein's highly controversial articles appeared quite often in the Annals.

3911

3981

At first these articles were mainly concerned with seeming contradictions in fact. Regarding movement, for instance, Albert pointed out that to a man standing in a field watching a train go by, the train obviously was passing the telegraph poles that lined the track. But to a man on the train, the poles would seem to be passing the train, proving that motion is relative to the observer.

4049

In an article concerning sound, Albert posed the following problem to his readers: When a man on a train traveling at sixty miles per hour blows a whistle, does the sound of the whistle travel 60 miles per hour faster than usual in the direction of the train and 60 miles per hour slower in the opposite direction? The answer was yes: to somebody on the ground the whistle's noise will travel at different speeds in these two directions. To the people on the train, however, the speed of the noise will be exactly the same as usual, because they themselves are moving with the whistle.

4155

In reading of past experiments, Albert found something very puzzling. While everything else fit into the above picture, the behavior of light was startlingly different.

Albert found that an experiment to test this question had been performed in 1887, by the American physicists Michelson and Morley. Try as they might, they could find no change in the speed of light even when the light source and observer were moving relative to one another. The speed of light, according to their measurements, is not relative – it is a constant of nature, always exactly the same no matter who is trying to determine it. 4257

This result was very surprising to the scientific world, which in those days thought that light traveled through a mysterious ether somewhat as sound travels through air. The nonexistence of an ether means that some very curious things can happen. Albert returned to his man on the moving train. Suppose that he stands in the very center of the train. To him, light from a match would reach both ends of the train at the same instant. But to someone standing on the ground, light from the match reaches the back of the train first, since it is "catching up" with the light, and only later on does it get to the front. Here is a case in which exactly the same thing appears very different indeed to different observers and this peculiar effect could not be predicted. 4395

Albert began reasoning with two definite notions: The basic laws of physics are the same whether there is a relative motion or not (things fall down on the train just as outside, objects have the same colors, and so on), is exactly the same to everybody, whether moving or not.

These two notions that Einstein adopted as the basis of his theory he called the Special Theory of Relativity. 4464

One of the first things that appeared in the theory was the prediction that moving objects become shortened and heavier than they would be if they were not moving relative to an observer. In other words, if we were to throw a ball fast enough – almost, but not quite, 186,000 miles per second – it would appear flattened and would weigh more than it did to start with. When it comes to a stop, its original size and weight reappear. According to Einstein, the closer the speed of some body gets to the speed of light, the closer its length becomes to zero and its weight to infinity. 4571

If a body were ever to travel with the speed of light it would have no size at all and an infinite mass, which is ridiculous; and so Einstein concluded that nothing could ever travel as fast as light or faster.

Even more astonishing was the result that even time is relative. Suppose we start out with two clocks, each exactly the same as the other. Now we can shoot one of them off in a rocket ship at a high speed. The clock in the rocket will appear to be slow with respect to the clock left behind! If the speed of the rocket ship is, say, 160,000 miles per second, its clock will tick once for every two clicks of the clock left behind. To somebody on the rocket ship, though, his clock will seem to tick "slower" than he would be if he had stayed on the ground. If our racketeer had left behind a twin brother, he would be younger than the twin when he returns to the earth after his voyage! 4747

These amazing, almost unbelievable conclusions that Albert Einstein was able to draw from his simple beginning were all eventually confirmed by experiments.

Still another conclusion of the Theory of Special Relativity has become the most famous of all. This is the fact that matter can be converted into energy, and energy into matter. We might take an atom of uranium, and cause it to break into two pieces in a laboratory experiment. When we do this, we find that the two pieces together weigh less than the original single uranium atom did – and that we now have a good deal of extra energy that we did not have before. The missing mass, m, had turned into an amount of energy E given by: 4834

$$E = mc^2$$

where c is the velocity of light. Because c is so large, and c^2 that much larger, even a minute amount of mass is equivalent to an immense amount of energy. This is the basic principle behind the operation of nuclear reactors – such as the ones that power atomic submarines and ships – and atomic bombs. These devices get their enormous energies from the conversion of mass into energy when uranium atoms are split. 4946

A closely related process takes place in the sun and other stars, where hydrogen atoms may be transformed, under conditions of great heat and pressure, into helium atoms. When this occurs, some mass is lost, and the resulting liberated energy causes the sun and stars to glow brightly. 4994

Surprising as it may seem, the reverse process also possible: energy can be changed into matter. There are found in nature some very high energy light waves called *gamma rays*, exactly the same as ordinary light except that we cannot see them. Gamma rays may be thought of as pure energy – they weigh nothing in the usual sense. When gamma rays pass near atoms, they often spontaneously turn into a pair of electrons, one with a positive electrical charge. And electrons most definitely *do* have mass. In this process, a gamma ray has *materialized* into a pair of electrons, with its energy having been turned into mass. 5101

Amazing as the creation of the Special Theory of Relativity was, Albert Einstein – still in his twenties – had another bombshell for physics in 1905, the year in which the work on relativity was published. This was the theory of the *photoelectric effect*, in its own way as daring as relativity. In fact, Einstein received the 1921 Nobel Prize in Physics for his work on the photo-electric effect, rather than on relativity. 5172

When light is shone on a metal surface, some electrons from the surface are emitted – they jump out. Curiously, the speed with which the electrons jump out depends upon the *color* of the light being used, and not on *how much* light there is. Blue light experiments showed faster electrons than red light. 5225

Einstein's radical explanation was that the energy carried in a beam of light is divided into tiny separate bits, called *photons*. The energy of each photon depends upon the frequency of the light; in other words, upon its color. The photons of blue light, which has a high frequency, carry more energy than the photons of red light, which has a lower frequency. Thus when a photon of blue light happens to hit an electron in a metal, it can give it more energy than a photon of red light, which exactly explained the observations. 5320

The concept that light has its energy in little packets is not at all easy to grasp. Thus his work was greeted with amazement and skepticism.

One day Albert walked into the office of the *Annalen der Physik*. He was, as usual, ushered in to see the editor.

"I have here a more than usually interesting article," Albert said. "It's about the possibility of releasing some of the energy that is imprisoned in certain masses of mineral matter."

5398

"I'm really very sorry, Herr Einstein," the editor replied. "You're just too late. The articles for the next issue have all been approved and sent to the printer. There just isn't room for another article. Perhaps in two months..."

"I feel that is should be published as quickly as possible," Albert persisted. "It contains descriptions of experiments on mass energy and a formula that will enable man to measure the energy in any mass."

5472

"Indeed," the editor said politely. "Well, well. But two months from now will do quite as well. It can't be so earth-shattering as all that."

"That's exactly what it is!" Albert explained.

"If you won't publish it immediately I'll have it printed myself and distribute it to every university. Since you've been publishing all my less important articles, it would make your periodical look rather foolish."

5538

"Very well, Einstein," the editor said quickly, "I'll pull one of the other articles and run yours."

However, instead of the vast explosion which Einstein had expected from the publication of his formula, $E=mc^2$, there resulted only the mildest of peeps. The ideas were just too great to be realized.

5588

Goal #2

Enstin
RPI
Hungary
Bugaria

4 students
swiss Polytec
learning laguay
4 students
one woman
study group

A girl was welcome
wanted to leave
teach poor in her country
Love making
she was accepted

Albert Einstein
By Arthur Beckhard

Chapter Two
"SHADOWS OF PREJUDICE"

Uncle Jacob's little game made a vast difference in Albert's work at school. As a matter of fact, it was responsible for much of his later success, for chasing the elusive "X" proved to have so great a fascination for him that mathematics soon became his favorite study. During the following year his marks improved amazingly, and he shot to the head of the class in algebra, geometry and physics.

Albert did not forget his promise to his parents. He never complained. But the hours spent in the classrooms of the Gymnasium seemed endless and, like the donkey whose master dangled a tempting morsel of new-mown hay just out of reach of his nose, Albert kept himself going from one class to the next by thinking of the fun that awaited him at home—books, talks, and his violin.   139

The wonderful evenings at the Einsteins' continued though a rival electrochemical shop was opened just across the street from the Einstein shop, just as Albert's father had foreseen. Business began to taper off. Some of their oldest customers admitted that they were afraid not to take their trade to the new store. They have been told it was owned by someone very high in political and army circles whose influence could be of benefit to them in many ways.

Hermann and Jacob Einstein had done so well for so long that they had been able to set aside quite a sum of money. At first they were not too concerned by the falling off of their profits. But as time passed and more and more of their customers deserted them, the partners knew something would have to be done before their savings disappeared. They began writing to friends and relatives in other cities and countries, asking if any of them knew of business opportunities.   303

Albert knew nothing of this, because his parents and Uncle Jacob were determined that their worries should not cast gloom over their cheerful evenings at home. So it came as a surprise when his parents told him that they were moving to Milan in Italy, where relatives had written to say there was a dry-goods and hardware store available.

It was even a greater shock to the boy when his parents told him that he could not go with them.   383

"You must finish your schooling so that you can get work, Albert," his father said. "I don't like to have the family separated and I don't like to think of you alone here in Munich, but there is no other way. You can stay at the Weills'. Their boy has gone into the army and they have a room. It will not be like staying with strangers."

"It will be for only a few months at a time," his mother added. "Your father will make enough money so that you will be able to spend the summer vacation with us."   483

"Of course," Albert said, smiling so that his mother would not cry. "I'll get along fine. It'll be fun being on my own."

He had promised that he would not complain about school and he meant to keep his word. But nobody was fooled. It was a sad day for all of them when Albert and Mr. and Mrs. Weill saw his family off on the little train that was to take them on the first lap of their journey.

563

Determined to concentrate on his schoolwork so that he could finish the course as quickly as possible, Albert neglected his violin. With every possible minute spent on study, the days passed more quickly than he had dared hope. He had no time for loneliness or self-pity. He did not go to Milan during the summer vacation. Instead, he studied at home in order to get ahead of his class in the hope of being able to skip a year.

There were bad days for Albert. His many questions angered his teachers because they seemed to show that he knew more than they did. He couldn't be punished for this but they were always on the lookout for ways of making him look silly in front of his classmates. Even this was not easy since, with his parents away and no friends or sports to distract him, there was nothing for him to do but study.

679

Perhaps that was why the teachers looked the other way and pretended not to hear when Albert's fellow students began making fun of him for being a Jew.

He had always known that his parents were Jewish, and that therefore he probably was too. But he had never thought about it very much or realized that it made him different from his fellow students.

His family, while deeply religious, were not followers of the Orthodox faith. They did not believe in the vengeful God of the Old Testament, but in the freedom and dignity of the individual and in the right of every man, woman, and child to worship God in whatever way he chooses.

794

He wished his parents were here so that he could ask them why the other boys and girls looked at him with such anger and bitterness. He wished he could ask them just what it meant to be a Jew. He couldn't ask the Weills. He could not think of an answer. This was not a case where he could call the unknown quantity "X" and seek its meaning in a formula.

He had promised his parents he would not complain, but this was different. He could feel the dislike of his classmates. They looked at him as if he had committed a crime. He would have to think of a way to get out of the Gymnasium and still have a chance of getting a diploma. He would keep his promise. He would not complain. And he would think of some means to be of help to his family; but he knew he would not continue in that school.

954

It was a dreary, depressing day. The rain, part sleet, slanted down on the windows of the train. There were five other passengers crowded into the stuffy compartment. There was every reason in the world why Albert should have been depressed, but he was not. To him the train might just as easily have been a golden chariot carrying him to the Royal Ball — or straight up into the clouds, for that matter. He was leaving Germany. Soon he would see his father and mother and Maja! He was going to Milan!

1046

For the hundredth time he looked around anxiously to make sure he still had his belongings. His lunch and supper? Yes — there on the floor under his feet. His clothes? That bulgy brown-paper parcel crowded into the luggage rack overhead. His books? He hoped he'd have no trouble getting the round-topped leather trunk from the baggage compartment in the car's vestibule. He clutched his violin in its wooden case and leaned his head back against the seat. He was actually on his way to Milan!   1131

As if he were reading about it in a book, he thought how this had been accomplished. It had been much simpler than he imagined once he had made up his mind to leave the school.

He had gone to the school physician and complained that he felt as if he were about to have violent fits. He would often dream of choking his ancient-history professor. As he had expected, the doctor reported the interview to the principal, and Albert had been summoned to the principal's office.   1218

He had been asked to wait in the anteroom. He had watched his teachers file in one after another to discuss his case with the principal. On the way out they had looked in his direction, some with pity, some in anger, but everyone with an expression of relief. When the principal had called him, his long face had been even more solemn than usual. He had told Albert that it had been decided to give him a certificate of ill-health; that in no way reflected on his standing as a student but that it meant he would be dismissed from the school. He was free to go to any other school or even to return here if he could pass the physical examination. He was free!   1345

He had hardly been able to keep from shouting it to the people on the streets. He had rushed to the Weills' house and written his father at once asking for the fare to Milan. He had said he was feeling fine, so that they would not worry.

Mr. Einstein had sent the money and here he was! He was going to see his mother and father, and he felt no sense of guilt. He knew that no one would have taken his "symptoms" seriously unless they'd been as eager to get rid of him as he had been to leave, and they had jumped at the first possible excuse offered. He grinned to himself in the crowded railway carriage.   1465

His family was overjoyed to see him. His mother exclaimed over and over again that he'd grown so tall she would not have recognized him. Maja too had grown and seemed surprisingly attractive to her big brother. His father and Uncle Jacob regarded him with undisguised pride. As a matter of fact, though he was unaware of it and would not have been interested in any case, he had grown into a very handsome boy with large dark eyes, brown wavy hair and look of great strength.   1552

One day he asked them why his fellow students had scorned him for being a Jew.

"We've often talked it over — your mother and Uncle Jacob and I," his father said.

"We've wondered whether we should warn you about the way so many people feel about Jews."

"You see, Albert," his mother said, "people really don't know why they feel that way. Some hold our religion against us. Others dislike us as a race."   1626

"We didn't tell you the whole truth in Munich, Albert," his father continued. "It was true that the army officers created competition to our store, but it was also true that our customers were told not to buy from us because we were Jews. That's why we came to Milan, where there is no prejudice against our people."

"It may be a good thing that this has happened when you are young, Albert," Uncle Jacob added. "It should teach you never to put labels on people because of their race, or the color of their skins. There are good people and bad people in every race. You must learn to judge each person for himself alone."

1637

"In other words," Mrs. Einstein finished, "try to be a fine man no matter what race you happen to belong to. We don't think of Mendelssohn as a great Jew. We think of him as a great composer. By the way, how do you intend to be great? Have you any plans?"

"Yes," Albert answered unhesitating. "I want to be a teacher."

"No more ideas of earning your living by playing the violin?" His father asked.

1713

"I want to prove that you can help people learn without punishing them," Albert said earnestly. "I want to try to get into Polytechnic Institute in Zurich, Switzerland."

"But that's run by the Swiss Government and admits only Swiss citizens," his mother said.

"Then I will become one. I don't want to be a German anymore. I don't believe it's right for a country to be run by soldiers and by force."

"Albert, you aren't old enough to be a citizen of any place," his mother spoke in laughter.

1802

"Then I'll wait," Albert answered. "Or perhaps when they see how much I know about mathematics they will make some special arrangement for me to get into Polytechnic. Anyway, I'm going to try."

1835

The last thing his parents wished was to shake Albert's self-confidence. They remembered only too well how shy he had been as a child, and they were glad to see that he was now ready to fight for what he believed in. So Mr. Einstein filled out the application for Albert to be allowed to take the entrance examinations to the great Polytechnic Institute which offered junior college courses, college courses and postgraduate work. To his surprise, his school record at the Munich Gymnasium won Albert the chance to take the exams.

Proudly, the family dipped into their savings to send their boy to Switzerland where he took all the necessary examinations. A week later the self-confident young man learned that he had flunked in biology, zoology and all languages.

1965

Chapter Three

PREPARATORY SCHOOL

Unlike his teachers at Munich Gymnasium, the professors at the Swiss Federal Polytechnic Institute in Zurich recognized in Albert the making of a great mathematician or physicist. Instead of discouraging him from further attempts to enter the great university, they suggested that he go to a preparatory school in Aarau, Switzerland, for at

2022

least a year. There he would be able to make up his deficiencies. Their belief in him gave him new courage. His failure to pass the entrance examinations seemed to him a challenge rather than a defeat. He sent in his application to the school at Aarau without even waiting to write home for advice, and to his great satisfaction, his application was accepted.

2086

He did not look forward to his term at Aarau with any pleasure, however. He fully expected to have to drill the dull rules of grammar into his head by endless repetition and grim determination. But he wrote home, packed his few belongings, and set out for the little village that backed up against the great Swiss Alps.

2144

To his amazement, nothing was as he had expected it to be. On the contrary the Aarau school gave Albert his first glimpse into what teaching could be like. He found complete freedom here. Students were enrolled at Aarau because they wanted to learn. The faculty was there to help those who needed it. The professors were not martinets. There was no feeling of military discipline. If someone wished to cut a class he cut it. No teacher rebuked him. But if he had difficulty in making up the lost classwork, no one sympathized with him; nor were the other, more conscientious students asked to suffer because of his absence. No lectures were repeated or reviewed. One attended class or had to make up the loss on one's own time.

2274

There was a much closer relationship between teacher and pupil than Albert had dreamed could exist. He was amazed to find that he was welcome as a guest in many faculty homes. It was in this way that he came to know and love the delightful Winteller family.

Whenever Albert went to visit them, he was reminded vividly of those beloved evenings at home in Munich. The Winteller family loved music as much as the Einsteins did. When Karl and Hans and Maria and the professor and Mrs. Winteller learned that Albert played the violin, he was urged to bring it to their house. Thereafter, they spent many evenings playing chamber music or singing ballads and Lieder, and Albert forgot his homesickness and had a wonderful time.

2401

His friendship with the Winteller family had many results. Mrs. Winteller saw to it, as his mother would have had she been there, that the tall, thin, growing boy got enough to eat. Karl, a boy of his own age, became his first friend. Professor Winteller himself was so convinced that Albert had a great deal to offer the world of science and would make an excellent teacher that he wrote about him not only to Mrs. Einstein but to his own friends. It was as a result of these letters that he discovered that an acquaintance of his was a prosperous and distant relative of the Einsteins. This gentleman began sending a little money each month to help Albert pay for his living expenses.

2467

2526

Unknown to the kind professor, Albert, instead of using this money to pay for food, clothing and laundry, began to do without socks or hats or overcoats and put aside as much as possible of this money toward the day when he would be old enough to become a Swiss citizen. He had learned that there was a registration fee that must accompany the application for citizenship, and he wanted to be sure that he would have enough money when the time came.

2609

It seemed to Albert that he had barely settle down when the year was over. It was difficult to say good-by to the Wintellers who had become such close friends. In all likelihood he would not see any of them soon again, for if he could pass his examinations in the fall, he would be living in Zurich, at a considerable distance from Aarau. Only a week before this unhappy parting, Albert had an inspiration.

"Karl, why don't you come to Milan with me for the summer?" he exclaimed.

"That'd be great, Albert, but — perhaps I'd better let you try to persuade Father." Albert was a convincing speaker, and professor Winteller gave his consent to the plan.

2726

In Milan, Albert was shocked to discover how thin and ill-looking his father had become. No one had written that Mr. Einstein's health had begun to fail, and that he could spend very little time in the shop. Nevertheless, in spite of their worries, the Einsteins all cheered upon the arrival of the two boys. It soon became apparent, even to Albert who was not very observant of such matters, that Karl was much taken with his little sister, Maja. For a time the three young people went everywhere together. They went to museums and for walks around the beautiful city. They even managed, by waiting in line, to get standing room at the opera for a few lire.

2845

It was a wonderful summer for Albert. He had never before had companions of his own age who liked the same things he liked. It was with real regret that he gradually came to realize that his sister and his friend did not always want him with them. When it finally dawned on him that they were in love, the summer was almost over.

One morning Karl went in to see Mr. Einstein alone. He told him he wanted to stay on in Milan and go into the Einstein business or at least help out at the store.

2943

"It isn't only that I've fallen in love with your daughter, Mr. Einstein," he explained. "I have, and I do want to stay here in Milan to be near her. But I know we're both too young to be married for some time, and that I must make money before I even ask her to become engaged."

"You seem to have thought of everything." Mr. Einstein said, stroking his mustache so as to hide a smile.

"There is something else. It's about Albert," Karl said.

3028

"He's worried about the money it will cost for him to go to the Swiss Federal Polytechnic. He sees that the business needs more help. He knows that you are not too well. He doesn't want to create hardships for all of you by leaving and..."

"Did he tell you this?"

"No, Mr. Einstein. Albert is going to be a great man some day. My father thinks so. The dean at Aarau thought so."

3102

"I think I know what you mean, Karl," Mr. Einstein said gravely. "I shall always remember something that happened when Albert was about five. He was just getting over the measles, and I used to bring him things to divert him. One day I happened to bring him a small compass. Nothing I had ever brought made so big a hit with him. He couldn't get enough of it.

3171

For months after he had recovered he carried it with him, asking questions of anyone who'd listen. What made the arrow move? What force was it that made it turn toward the north? What was magnetism? What was gravity? It was, as you just said, as if he was trying to understand the whole universe — at five."

3228

"You know, then, how important it is that he go to the Swiss Federal Polytechnic Institute — one of the greatest of its sort in the world?"

Mr. Einstein nodded. "I'll be proud to accept your offer to take his place here, Karl. It will be fine to have you with us. And I'm sure Maja will be delighted." Mr. Einstein smiled warmly on his prospective son-in-law.

Albert knew nothing of this. He only knew that the whole family escorted him to see him off when the time came for him to leave for Zurich, and that they all disguised the sorrow of parting by expressing the highest hopes for his success. They knew he would succeed.

3344

1. Uncle Jacob's game of chasing the elusive "X": (70 words)
    a. improved Albert's marks amazingly.
    b. provided just a brief fascination for Albert.
    c. became so fascinating for Albert that his grades suffered.
    d. seemed childish to Albert.

2. Albert's family moved to Milan: (364 words)
    a. to find a better climate.
    b. so Mrs. Einstein could be near relatives.
    c. because of falling profits due to pressure from the army.
    d. so they could afford to send Albert to a better school.

3. After Albert's family left for Milan, he stayed: (580 words)
    a. with the Weills', friends of the Einsteins.
    b. at the boarding school.
    c. with his uncle.
    d. with his father's parents.

4. Albert concentrated on his schoolwork: (712 words)
    a. to further demonstrate his abilities to his teachers.
    b. so he could finish the course as quickly as possible and perhaps skip a year.
    c. to rapidly learn more about his favorite subjects.
    d. to spite his teachers.

5. Albert was dismissed from school: (1,437 words)
    a. with a certificate of ill-health.
    b. because of poor grades.
    c. due to his constant complaining.
    d. because his parents ran out of money.

6. After Albert arrived in Milan, his parents noticed: (1,630 words)
    a. that he had grown thin.
    b. that he talked a great deal about his studies.
    c. that he looked worried despite his excitement.
    d. that he had grown tall, handsome, and strong.

7. Albert told his parents he wanted to be a chemist. (1,900 words)
    T   F

8. When Albert attended preparatory school in Switzerland: (2,480 words)
    a. he found hints of the same military discipline he had encountered in Germany.
    b. he was amazed to find school enjoyable.
    c. he began to realize why his classmates didn't like him.
    d. he was still unable to get close to his teachers.

9. What was the name of Albert's new friend who went home to Milan with him for the summer? (2,882 words)
    a. Maria
    b. Karl
    c. Hans
    d. Marcel

10. Mr. Einstein's health began to fail to the point where he could spend very little time in the shop. (2,960 words)
    T   F

ACTIVITY	DAY	TIME

Week 1

Read a trade journal using the entire Dynamic Reading process.

——— ———

Devote 15 minutes per day to intense, uninterrupted reading of materials that are of professional or personal interest.

——— ———

Three times during the week perform the following activity:

Practice the hand patterns (see page 7 in the workbook) appropriate to each speed range for 20 minutes:

4 to 5 seconds/page	5 minutes
6 to 8 seconds/page	5 minutes
9 to 12 seconds/page	5 minutes
13 to 16 seconds/page	5 minutes

——— ———

Listen to one television news broadcast. Take notes on a Slash Recall Pattern.

——— ———

ACTIVITY	DAY	TIME

Week 2

Read a trade journal using the entire Dynamic Reading process.

——— ———

Use a Recall Pattern in every meeting you attend.

——— ———

Practice the Push-Up Drill three times. Record rate and estimate comprehension on chart.

——— ———

Read a book about something you have wanted to learn more about using the entire dynamic reading process.

——— ———

QUOTABLES

"Psychologist William James suggested that to change personal habits, we first make a deep internal commitment to pay whatever price is necessary to change the habit; second, we grasp the very first opportunity to use the new practice or skill; and third, we allow no exceptions until the new habit is firmly imbedded into our nature."

Stephen R. Covey
Principle-Centered Leadership

ACTIVITY	DAY	TIME

Week 3

Dynamically read one book that you know a non-Dynamic Reader has read. Get together with that person and openly discuss that book.

———— ————

Fully read two magazines and journals that you have wanted to read, using the entire Dynamic Reading process.

———— ————

Practice the Push-Up Drill three times. Record rate and estimate comprehension on chart.

———— ————

ACTIVITY	DAY	TIME

Week 4

Use a Recall Pattern while taking notes from all phone conversations.

———— ————

Use the entire Dynamic Reading process to go through your entire in-box. Be sure to use the marking system.

———— ————

Practice the Push-Up Drill three times. Record rate and estimate comprehension on chart.

———— ————

Read a trade journal using the entire Dynamic Reading process.

———— ————

QUOTABLES

"In the early stages of acquiring any really new skill, a person must adopt at least a partly antipleasure attitude: "Good, this is a change to experience awkwardness and to discover new kinds of mistakes!" It is the same for doing mathematics, climbing freezing mountain peaks, or playing pipe organs with one's feet. Some parts of the mind find it horrible, while other parts enjoy forcing those first parts to work for them."

Marvin Minsky
The Society of Mind

	DAY	TIME	RATE	COMP.
Week 2				
Week 3				
Week 4				

Steps for Practicing the Push-Up Drill

Task	Time
1. Read for Level 3 Comprehension.	1 Minute
2. Reread from the beginning – faster and farther.	1 Minute
3. Reread from the beginning – faster and farther.	1 Minute
4. Reread from the beginning – double the length of 3.	1 Minute
5. Reread from the beginning – triple the length of 3.	1 Minute
6. Read from the end of 3.	1 Minute
7. Write whatever you can recall on a Recall Pattern.	1 Minute
8. Calculate words per minute (WPM) for 6.	

1.
2.
3.
4.
5.
6.
7. Create Recall Pattern.
8. Calculate words per minute (WPM) for 6.

When practicing with the Push-Up Drill, use some type of a timer. Accuracy is not as important as having a bell or timer to indicate when to stop. Looking at a stopwatch or wristwatch is distracting. Try a digital kitchen timer or talk into a tape recorder saying "begin," watching a timing device for one minute, and then saying "stop."

Tips to Remember

♦ Try to practice on material a little lower than your current reading level.

♦ Continue to experiment with a variety of hand motions.

♦ Keep in mind that for the first 5 steps, you're drilling – stretching yourself. It's okay not to "get it all."

... in your own material

To determine the average words per line (WPL):

- Count the number of words on three (or six) full lines.

- Divide that number of words by three (or six) to get the average words per line (WPL).

To determine the average words per page (WPP):

- Count the number of lines on a full page (LPP).

- Multiply the WPL by the number of lines per page (LPP) to get the approximate number of words per page (WPP).

To determine total words:

- Multiply the number of full pages read during the timed drill by the WPP.

- Count the extra lines.

- Multiply the number of extra lines by the WPL.

- Add the WPP and the WPL totals together to get **Total Words**.

To find your average words per minute (WPM):

Divide the **Total Words** by the **Time** (number of minutes you read) to get the WPM.

$$\text{WPM} = \frac{\textbf{Total Words}}{\textbf{Time}}$$

PUSH-DOWN DRILL (for comprehension)

Read at Level 3 (Preview) for	1 minute
Re-preview same material for	45 seconds
Re-preview same material for	30 seconds
Re-preview same material for	20 seconds

Go to New Material

Read at Level 3 (Preview) for	1 minute
Read at Level 4 (same material)	30 seconds
Do a Recall Pattern on what you read	1 minute
Calculate WPM	_____ WPM

Potential Challenge	Coaching Tips
I'm occasionally distracted by my own consciousness of subvocalizing and my efforts to reduce it.	In the early stages of learning to read dynamically, this is quite normal. Remember "bypassing subvocalization" does not mean a silent mind. Dynamic Reading means filling your mind with unique thoughts based on some of the words you see. ♦ While reading at high speeds work to "springboard" off of words you see to make mental pictures. These thoughts and pictures will gradually overlap more and more of your subvocalization as you practice. (i.e., push up drills)
Occasionally I feel like my hand distracts me. I sometimes find myself thinking about my hand.	♦ Occasionally practice on material that you find especially interesting or fascinating. Your interest will help focus you past your hand, enabling you to feel more comfortable with it as a reading tool. ♦ While also remaining flexible, try to get "used to" the hand motions you find most helpful. Your comfort with them will reduce your distraction.
I'm not recreating information on a recall pattern as well as I'd like to be. I find myself writing ideas word for word or writing too much.	♦ Don't feel rushed as you create recall patterns, especially in the early stages of practice. Feel free to take a moment before you write each item to specifically rephrase it in your own words. Soon, as you read, you will find "rephrased" thoughts popping into your mind which you can more immediately record on your recall patterns.
It seems like I'm taking more time to create recall patterns than I should.	♦ Set aside specific time to practice simply the mechanics of drawing the types of recall patterns you feel most comfortable with. ♦ Whether you get thoughts instantly as you read or you're practicing "translating" the author's words as mentioned above, try to reduce the thought to as few words as possible. Then, make sure you go back after some time to test how well these phrases trigger the depth of the thought you had. You may be surprised after some practice.
I don't feel like I'm getting enough meaning from material when I'm moving at faster speeds with hand motions other than underline.	Remember, reading extremely fast with excellent comprehension takes a great deal of practice. ♦ As you practice the Multiple Reading Process, spend much more time previewing material, thoroughly familiarizing yourself with it but not fully reading it. Your familiarity, just as in a Push-Up drill, will enable you to experience "how it feels" as you read at much higher speeds with solid comprehension. You can then gradually reduce the amount of preview time and challenge yourself.
I'm using dynamic reading techniques well, but occasionally I feel like I get "bogged down" in certain types of heavier reading.	♦ Usually the feeling of getting "bogged down" is a signal that you need to preview over a smaller section of material to identify ideas. ♦ Concentrate on "layering" your reading and thinking. The context for material generated by prereading can often be the most useful thing to help you understand more clearly and "move on."

Potential Challenge	Coaching Tips
I'm not as confident using dynamic reading techniques with technical, detailed, or high responsibility material.	Actually, some of this apprehension may come more from your overall perception of the "heaviness" of technical material. Actually, technical and highly-detailed material is among the best organized and most logically presented material you can find. ♦ Use the Multiple Reading Process to take advantage of its structure. ♦ Divide the material into smaller segments and concentrate more on layering—preview twice, post-view twice, return to your recall often.
I'm occasionally finding myself wanting to read straight through material without an overview or preview.	Remember, how you choose to apply the tools of the Multiple Reading Process depends on your purpose. If you find yourself "diving straight into" reading material, use that simply as a cue to reflect on your purpose for reading the material. Many times your purpose will point you to spend time prereading. But, if you're reading a novel to fall asleep, you may choose to slowly enjoy the book. Flexibility according to purpose is key.
I'm using the Dynamic Reading skills confidently, but I'm still not reading quite as fast as I'd like to be.	♦ Concentrate as you practice on continually seeing words faster than you can see them comfortably. This is called sensory overload drilling. Train yourself to see words faster (the physical component of reading) and then when you slow your speeds down to read (the mental side of reading) you will be faster than before. ♦ Fill your practice time with more Push-Up drills on more of a variety of reading material. ♦ Be sure not to confuse high-speed practice (rapid rates with minimal comprehension) with reading (comprehension according to your purpose) or you will be frustrated.
I'm still a little confused as to where my eyes should focus when I use the various hand motions.	Remember, when you read extremely difficult material, use the underline hand motion where your eyes stay right with your finger tip and your hand almost follows your eye to ensure you are going slow enough to match your purpose. Hand motions are an accompaniment to your thoughtful reading and simply provide rhythm, pace and purposeful motion for your eye. However, with all hand motions other than underline, your eye will not directly follow your hand. Your eyes should move over the page to see words and generate thoughts which fulfill your purpose.
As my eyes move from right to left, I feel like I'm comprehending less than I should be.	Experienced Dynamic Readers are so busy thinking about content that they are not even aware of any specific right to left movement of the eyes. They are simply trying to see more words to continue their thinking. Initially, as you are focusing more on the process itself, right to left eye movement may be distracting. ♦ Practice more with narrow column material and gradually expand your practice with wider columns. The author's thoughts and phrases are more closely linked in narrow columns, making right to left movement less uncomfortable.

What You Need for This Lesson:

Evelyn Wood Course Guide

Audio CD #1

Pencil or pen

DO NOT TURN TO THE NEXT
PAGE UNTIL INSTRUCTED TO
DO SO ON THE AUDIO CD.

Lesson 1

Find Your Present Reading Rate

Evelyn Wood
READING DYNAMICS®

The Boys' Life of Abraham Lincoln
by Helen Nicolay

The Man Who Was President

The way Mr. Lincoln signed this most important state paper was thoroughly in keeping with his nature. He hated all shams and show and pretense, and being absolutely without affectation of any kind, it would never have occurred to him to pose for effect while signing the Emancipation Proclamation or any other paper. He never thought of himself as a President to be set up before a multitude and admired, but always as a President charged with duties which he owed to every citizen. In fulfilling these he did not stand upon ceremony, but took the most direct way to the end he had in view.   106

It is not often that a President pleads a cause before Congress. Mr. Lincoln did not find it beneath his dignity at one time to go in person to the Capitol, and calling a number of the leading senators and representatives around him, explain to them, with the aid of a map, his reasons for believing that the final stand of the Confederates would be made in that part of the South where the seven States of Virginia, North Carolina, South Carolina, Georgia, Tennessee, Kentucky and West Virginia come together; and strive in this way to interest them in the sad plight of the loyal people of Tennessee who were being persecuted by the Confederate government, but whose mountainous region might, with a little help, be made a citadel of Union strength in the very heart of this stronghold of rebellion.   247

In his private life he was entirely simple and unaffected. Yet he had a deep sense of what was due his office, and took part with becoming dignity in all official or public ceremonies. He received the diplomats sent to Washington from the courts of Europe with a formal and quiet reserve which made them realize at once that although this son of the people had been born in a log cabin, he was ruler of a great nation, and more than that, was a prince by right of his own fine instincts and good breeding.   343

He was ever gentle and courteous, but with a few quiet words he could silence a bore who had come meaning to talk to him for hours. For his friends he had always a ready smile and a quaintly turned phrase. His sense of humor was his salvation. Without it he must have died of the strain and anxiety of the Civil War. There was something almost pathetic in the way he would snatch a moment from his pressing duties and gravest cares to listen to a good story or indulge in a hearty laugh. Some people could not understand this. To one member of his cabinet, at least, it seemed strange and unfitting that he should read aloud to them a chapter from a humorous   469
book by Artemus Ward before taking up the weighty matter of the Emancipation Proclamation. From their point of view it showed lack of feeling and frivolity of character, when, in truth, it was the very depth of his feeling, and the intensity of his distress at the suffering of the war, that led him to seek relief in laughter, to gather from the comedy of life strength to go on and meet its sternest tragedy.   544

He was a social man. He could not fully enjoy even a jest alone. He wanted somebody to share the pleasure with him. Often when care kept him awake late at night he would wander through the halls of the Executive Mansion, and coming to the room where his secretaries were still at work, would stop to read to them some poem, or a passage from Shakespeare, or a bit from one of the humorous books in which he found relief. No one knew better than he what could be cured, and what must be   639 patiently endured. To every difficulty that he could remove he gave cheerful and uncomplaining thought and labor. The burdens he could not shake off he bore with silent courage, lightening them whenever possible with the laughter that he once described as the "universal joyous evergreen of life."

686

It would be a mistake to suppose that he cared only for humorous reading. Occasionally he read a scientific book with great interest, but his duties left him little time for such indulgences. Few men knew the Bible more thoroughly than he did, and his speeches are full of scriptural quotations. The poem beginning "Oh, why should the spirit of mortal be proud?" was one of his favorites, and Dr. Holmes's "Last Leaf" was another. Shakespeare was his constant delight. A copy of Shakespeare's works was even to be found in the busy Executive Office, from which most books were banished. The President not only liked to read the great poet's plays, but to see them acted; and when the gifted actor Hackett came to Washington, he was invited to the White House, where the two discussed the character of Falstaff, and the proper reading of many scenes and passages.

836

While he was President, Mr. Lincoln did not attempt to read the newspapers. His days were long, beginning early and ending late, but they were not long enough for that. One of his secretaries brought him a daily memorandum of the important news they contained. His mail was so enormous that he personally read only about one in every hundred of the letters sent him.

901

His time was principally taken up with interviews with people on matters of importance, with cabinet meetings, conferences with his generals, and other affairs requiring his close and immediate attention. If he had leisure he would take a drive in the late afternoon, or perhaps steal away into the grounds south of the Executive Mansion to test some new kind of gun, if its inventor had been fortunate enough to bring it to his notice. He was very quick to understand mechanical contrivances, and would often suggest improvements that had not occurred to the inventor himself.

997

For many years it has been the fashion to call Mr. Lincoln homely. He was very tall, and very thin. His eyes were deep-sunken, his skin of a sallow pallor, his hair coarse, black, and unruly. Yet he was neither ungraceful, nor awkward, nor ugly. His large features fitted his large frame, and his large hands and feet were but right on a body that measured six feet four inches. His was a sad and thoughtful face, and from boyhood he had carried a load of care. It was small wonder that when alone, or absorbed in thought, the face should take on deep lines, the eyes appear as if seeing something beyond the vision of other men, and the shoulders stoop, as though they too were bearing a weight. But in a moment all would be changed. The deep eyes could flash, or twinkle merrily with humor, or look out from under overhanging brows as they did upon the Five Points children in kindliest gentleness. In public speaking, his tall body rose to its full height, his head was thrown back, his face seemed transfigured with the fire and earnestness of his thought, and his voice took on a high clear tenor tone that carried his words and ideas far out over the listening crowds. At such moments, when answering Douglas in the heat of their joint-debate, or later, during the years of war, when he pronounced with noble gravity the words of his famous addresses, not one in the throngs that heard him could say with truth that he was other than a handsome man.

1122

1264

It has been the fashion, too, to say that he was slovenly, and careless in his dress. This also is a mistake. His clothes could not fit smoothly on his gaunt and bony frame. He was no tailor's figure of a man; but from the first he clothed himself as well as his means allowed, and in the fashion of the time and place. In reading the grotesque stories of his boyhood, of the tall stripling whose trousers left exposed a length of shin, it must be remembered not only how poor he was, but that he lived on the frontier, where other boys, less poor, were scarcely better clad. In Vandalia, the blue jeans he wore was the dress of his companions as well, and later, from Springfield days on, clear through his presidency, his costume was the usual suit of black broadcloth, carefully made, and scrupulously neat. He cared nothing for style. It did not matter to him whether the man with whom he talked wore a coat of the latest cut, or owned no coat at all. It was the man inside the coat that interested him.

1377

1454

In the same way he cared little for the pleasures of the table. He ate most sparingly. He was thankful that food was good and wholesome and enough for daily needs, but he could no more enter into the mood of the epicure for whose palate it is a matter of importance whether he eats roast goose or golden pheasant, than he could have counted the grains of sand under the sea.

1526

In the summers, while he was President, he spent the nights at a cottage at the Soldiers' Home, a short distance north of Washington, riding or driving out through the gathering dusk, and returning to the White House after a frugal breakfast in the early morning. Ten o'clock was the hour at which he was supposed to begin receiving visitors, but it was often necessary to see them unpleasantly early. Occasionally they forced their way to his bedroom before he had quite finished dressing. Throngs of people daily filled his office, the ante-rooms, and even the corridors of the public part of the Executive Mansion. He saw them all, those he had summoned on important business, men of high official position who came to demand as their right offices and favors that he had no right to give; others who wished to offer tiresome if well-meant advice; and the hundreds, both men and women, who pressed forward to ask all sorts of help. His friends besought him to save himself the weariness of seeing the people at these public receptions, but he refused. "They do not want much, and they get very little," he answered. "Each one considers his business of great importance, and I must gratify them. I know how I would feel if I were in their place." And at noon on all days except Tuesday and Friday, when the time was occupied by meetings of the cabinet, the doors were thrown open, and all who wished might enter. That remark of his, "I know how I would feel if I were in their place," explained it all. His early experience of life had drilled him well for these ordeals. He had read deeply in the book of human nature, and could see the hidden signs of falsehood and deceit and trickery from which the faces of some of his visitors were not free; but he knew, too, the hard, practical side of life, the hunger, cold, storms, sickness and misfortune that the average man must meet in his struggle with the world. More than all, he knew and sympathized with that hope deferred which makes the heart sick.

1656

1780

1887

***

Mr. Lincoln sympathized keenly with the hardships and trials of the soldier boys, and found time, amid all his labors and cares, to visit the hospitals in and around Washington where they lay ill. His afternoon drive was usually to some camp in the neighborhood of the city; and when he visited one at a greater distance, the cheers that greeted him as he rode along the line with the commanding general showed what a warm place he held in their hearts.

1970

He did not forget the unfortunate on these visits. A story is told of his interview with William Scott, a boy from a Vermont farm, who, after marching forty-eight hours without sleep, volunteered to stand guard for a sick comrade. Weariness overcame him, and he was found asleep at his post, within gunshot of the enemy. He was tried, and sentenced to be shot. Mr. Lincoln heard of the case, and went himself to the tent where young Scott was kept under guard. He talked to him kindly, asking about his home, his schoolmates, and particularly about his mother. The lad took her picture from his pocket, and showed it to him without speaking. Mr. Lincoln was much affected. As he rose to leave he laid his hand on the prisoner's shoulder. "My boy," he said, "you are not going to be shot to-morrow. I believe you when you tell me that you could not keep awake. I am going to trust you, and send you back to your regiment. Now, I want to know what you intend to pay for all this?" The lad, overcome with gratitude, could hardly say a word, but crowding down his emotions, managed to answer that he did not know. He and his people were poor, they would do what they could. There was his pay, and a little in the savings bank. They could borrow something by a mortgage on the farm. Perhaps his comrades would help. If Mr. Lincoln would wait until pay day possibly they might get together five or six hundred dollars. Would that be enough? The kindly President shook his head. "My bill is a great deal more than that," he said. "It is a very large one. Your friends cannot pay it, nor your family, nor your farm. There is only one man in the world who can pay it, and his name is William Scott. If from this day he does his duty so that when he comes to die he can truly say "I have kept the promise I gave the President. I have done my duty as a soldier,' then the debt will be paid." Young Scott went back to his regiment, and the debt was fully paid a few months later, for he fell in battle.

2088

2216

2352

Mr. Lincoln's own son became a soldier after leaving college. The letter his father wrote to General Grant in his behalf shows how careful he was that neither his official position nor his desire to give his boy the experience he wanted, should work the least injustice to others:

Executive Mansion,

Washington, January 19th, 1865.

Lieutenant-General Grant:

Please read and answer this letter as though I was not President, but only a friend. My son, now in his twenty-second year, having graduated at Harvard, wishes to see something of the war before it ends. I do not wish to put him in the ranks, nor yet to give him a commission, to which those who have already served long are better entitled, and better qualified to hold. Could he, without embarrassment to you, or detriment to the service, go into your military family with some nominal rank, I and not the public furnishing the necessary means? If no, say so without the least hesitation, because I am as anxious and as deeply interested that you shall not be encumbered as you can be yourself.

2439

Yours truly,

A. Lincoln.

2540

His interest did not cease with the life of a young soldier. Among his most beautiful letters are those he wrote to sorrowing parents who had lost their sons in battle; and when his personal friend, young Ellsworth, one of the first and most gallant to fall, was killed at Alexandria, the President directed that his body be brought to the White House, where his funeral was held in the great East Room.

2613

***

Children held a warm place in the President's affections. He was not only a devoted father; his heart went out to all little folk. He had been kind to babies in his boyish days, when, book in hand, and the desire for study upon him, he would sit with one foot on the rocker of a rude frontier cradle, not too selfishly busy to keep its small occupant lulled and content, while its mother went about her household tasks. After he became President many a sad-eyed woman carrying a child in her arms went to see him, and the baby always had its share in gaining her a speedy hearing, and if possible a favorable answer to her petition.

2732

When children came to him at the White House of their own accord, as they sometimes did, the favors they asked were not refused because of their youth. One day a small boy, watching his chance, slipped into the Executive Office between a governor and a senator, when the door was opened to admit them. They were as much astonished at seeing him there as the President was, and could not explain his presence; but he spoke for himself. He had come, he said, from a little country town, hoping to get a place as page in the House of Representatives. The President began to tell him that he must go to Captain Goodnow, the doorkeeper of the House, for he himself had nothing to do with such appointments. Even this did not discourage the little fellow. Very earnestly he pulled his papers of recommendation out of his pocket, and Mr. Lincoln, unable to resist his wistful face, read them, and sent him away happy with a hurried line written on the back of them, saying: "If Captain Goodnow can give this good little boy a place, he will oblige A. Lincoln."

2837

2924

It was a child who persuaded Mr. Lincoln to wear a beard. Up to the time he was nominated for President he had always been smooth-shaven. A little girl living in Chautauqua County, New York, who greatly admired him, made up her mind that he would look better if he wore whiskers, and with youthful directness wrote and told him so. He answered her by return mail:

2991

Springfield, ILL., Oct. 19, 1860.
Miss Grace Bedelt,

My dear little Miss: Your very agreeable letter of the fifteenth is received. I regret the necessity of saying I have no daughter. I have three sons, one seventeen, one nine, and one seven years of age. They, with their mother, constitute my whole family. As to the whiskers, never having worn any, do you not think people would call it a piece of silly affectation if I were to begin now?

Your very sincere well-wisher,
A. Lincoln.

3077

Evidently on second thoughts he decided to follow her advice. On his way to Washington his train stopped at the town where she lived. He asked if she were in the crowd gathered at the station to meet him. Of course she was, and willing hands forced a way for her through the mass of people. When she reached the car Mr. Lincoln stepped from the train, kissed her, and showed her that he had taken her advice.

3155

The Secretary who wrote about the President's desire to save the lives of condemned soldiers tells us that "during the first year of the administration the house was made lively by the games and pranks of Mr. Lincoln's two younger children, William and Thomas. Robert the eldest was away at Harvard, only coming home for short vacations. The two little boys, aged eight and ten, with their western independence and enterprise, kept the house in an uproar. They drove their tutor wild with their

3239

good-natured disobedience. They organized a minstrel show in the attic; they made acquaintance with the office-seekers and became the hot champions of the distressed. William was, with all his boyish frolic, a child of great promise, capable of close application and study. He had a fancy for drawing up railway time-tables, and would conduct an imaginary train from Chicago to New York with perfect precision. He wrote childish verses, which sometimes attained the unmerited honors of print. But this bright, gentle and studious child sickened and died in February, 1862. His father was profoundly moved by his death, though he gave no outward sign of his trouble, but kept about his work, the same as ever. His bereaved heart seemed afterwards to pour out its fullness on his youngest child. 'Tad' was a merry, warm-blooded, kindly little boy, perfectly lawless, and full of odd fancies and inventions, the 'chartered libertine' of the Executive Mansion." He ran constantly in and out of his father's office, interrupting his gravest labors. Mr. Lincoln was never too busy to hear him, or to answer his bright, rapid, imperfect speech, for he was not able to speak plainly until he was nearly grown. "He would perch upon his father's knee, and sometimes even on his shoulder, while the most weighty conferences were going on. Sometimes, escaping from the domestic authorities, he would take refuge in that sanctuary for the whole evening, dropping to sleep at last on the floor, when the President would pick him up, and carry him tenderly to bed."

3374

3497

The letters and even the telegrams Mr. Lincoln sent his wife had always a message for or about Tad. One of them shows that his pets, like their young master, were allowed great liberty. It was written when the family was living at the Soldiers' Home, and Mrs. Lincoln and Tad had gone away for a visit. "Tell dear Tad," he wrote, "that poor Nanny Goat is lost, and Mrs. Cuthbert and I are in distress about it. The day you left, Nanny was found resting herself and chewing her little cud on the middle of Tad's bed; but now she's gone! The gardener kept complaining that she destroyed the flowers, till it was concluded to bring her down to the White House. This was done, and the second day she had disappeared and has not been heard of since. This is the last we know of poor Nanny."

3646

Tad was evidently consoled by, not one, but a whole family of new goats, for about a year later Mr. Lincoln ended a business telegram to his wife in New York with the words: "Tell Tad the goats and Father are very well." Then, as the weight of care rolled back upon this greathearted, patient man, he added, with humorous weariness, "especially the goats."

3710

Mr. Lincoln was so forgetful of self as to be absolutely without personal fear. He not only paid no attention to the threats which were constantly made against his life, but when, on July 11, 1864, the Confederate General Early appeared suddenly and unexpectedly before the city with a force of 17,000 men, and Washington was for two days actually in danger of assault and capture, his unconcern gave his friends great uneasiness. On the tenth he rode out, as was his custom, to spend the night at the Soldiers' Home, but Secretary Stanton, learning that Early was advancing, sent after him, to compel his return. Twice afterward, intent upon watching the fighting which took place near Fort Stevens, north of the city, he exposed his tall form to the gaze and bullets of the enemy, utterly heedless of his own peril; and it was not until an officer had fallen mortally wounded within a few feet of him, that he could be persuaded to seek a place of greater safety.

3881

If you finish early...

If you finish reading the passage before the tone sounds, IMMEDIATELY BEGIN TIMING the amount of time left until the tone sounds. To compute your reading rate:

♦ Round off the amount of time you did not use to the nearest quarter minute. For example, 11 seconds would be ¼ minute.

♦ Subtract the amount of time you did not use from three minutes to find the amount of time you did use.

♦ Divide the total number of words (3881) by the amount of time you used.

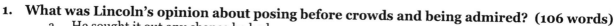

1. **What was Lincoln's opinion about posing before crowds and being admired?** (106 words)
   a. He sought it out any chance he had.
   b. He grew to enjoy it.
   c. He hated it and chose to focus on his duties.
   d. He felt embarrassed and unworthy of the honor.

2. **Why did President Lincoln go in person to Congress to plead his case?** (247 words)
   a. To discuss strategy about the final stand of the Confederates
   b. To get the Emancipation Proclamation signed
   c. To declare war on the South
   d. To deliver the Gettysburg Address

3. **What did Lincoln often do before discussing a serious subject?** (544 words)
   a. Meditate in the rose garden
   b. Read a selection from a funny book or listen to a joke
   c. Call in his most trusted advisors
   d. Call in people that he knew would have opposing opinions

4. **What did Lincoln often do when he couldn't sleep?** (686 words)
   a. Sit up in bed and read
   b. Go down to the Oval Office and work
   c. Wander through the White House until he found someone to talk to
   d. Play the piano

5. **What did Lincoln often do if he had a little bit of leisure time?** (997 words)
   a. Write letters to friends
   b. Play cards
   c. Take a drive
   d. Listen to the radio

6. **Which statement best describes Lincoln's eating habits?** (1526 words)
   a. He enjoyed fine dining, especially pheasant.
   b. He had severe allergies that restricted his diet.
   c. He refused to eat alone, and would only eat with friends.
   d. He ate sparingly and simply.

7. **What did Lincoln do at noon on most days?** (1777 words)
   a. Take a nap
   b. Open his doors to see anyone who wanted time with him
   c. Spend an hour in the residence catching up on his correspondence
   d. Walk one lap around the grounds of the White House

8. **What did Lincoln ask in return of the soldier he pardoned?** (2352 words)
   a. That he fulfill his duty
   b. That he donate one pay check to charity
   c. That he write to his family so they'd know he was OK
   d. That he write a formal apology

9. **What did the little boy who snuck into the Executive Office want?** (2925 words)
   a. A pardon for his father
   b. To join the military
   c. A piece of his beard
   d. A job as a page

10. **What kind of pets did Tad have?** (3646 words)
    a. Snakes
    b. Horses
    c. Dogs
    d. Goats

Calculating Comprehension Scores

Number of Questions Responsible for Answering

Number of Questions Correct	1	2	3	4	5	6	7	8	9	10
1	100	50	33	25	20	16	14	13	11	10
2		100	67	50	40	33	29	25	22	20
3			100	75	60	50	43	38	33	30
4				100	80	67	57	50	44	40
5					100	83	72	63	56	50
6						100	86	75	67	60
7							100	88	78	70
8								100	89	80
9									100	90
10										100

Pre-Session Summary

Words Per Minute Rate:

Comprehension Score

Write major points in the column on the left and details or supporting points in the column on the right.

More Important Points	Details & Supporting Points
Jack and Jill climb hill	
	for water
Jack falls	
	breaks "crown"
	Jill tumbles, too

EXAMPLE

Write everything you remember from the selection you have read. Do NOT look back at the reading. Write only one item on each line.

More Important Points	Details & Supporting Points

Go on to the next page if you need more room.

More Important Points	Details & Supporting Points

Total number of Important Points: _____

Total number of Supporting Points: _____

Could you have written more with more time? _____

Average words per minute reading rate: _____

What You Need for This Lesson:

Evelyn Wood Course Guide

Audio CD #1

Pencil or pen

An easy novel or biography of your choice

Lesson 2

*Increase Your Reading
Speed Immediately*

**Evelyn Wood
READING DYNAMICS®**

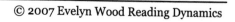

Years ago when I was much younger and bolder, I was so frustrated by my own slow reading that I determined to teach myself to read faster and better, then try to teach high school students what I had learned to do for myself. I studied the reading authorities. I read their definitions of reading and found they could not agree how to define reading or comprehension so they made up their own definitions to fit their own needs. I studied the experiments of Cattell and Buswell and many others in the field. I became confused. The educational literature contains such references as: In the May 1950 issue of *Education,* Elizabeth Simpson is quoted as saying, "Of course, no one would assume that while the tachistoscopic studies show we can recognize a word at 1/100th of a second, it is also true we can read 6,000 words in a minute. We know we can't recognize so many ideas so quickly." I began to think—what if the 6,000 words represented only one or two ideas? Would this make a difference? It is in the field where we know things can't be done that so much is being done. Some authorities assured me reading must be done along the line, seeing most of the words; and that span is horizontal, making the idea situation two or three fixations along the line. Nila Banton Smith, in her book *Read Faster,* page 244, says, "We fixate at a point along the line and see all the words we can see to the left and right of the fixation, then move on to another fixation and repeat the perception process." Then she adds this observation: "But it happens that we also possess a vertical field of vision which usually lies dormant insofar as reading is concerned." I wondered why someone didn't do something to explore the potentialities of this field.

W-A-T-E-R

by Lorena A. Hickock

The day had got off to a bad start. It was April 5th, just two days over a month since The Stranger had come to be Helen's teacher.

Because Captain Keller had insisted on it, Helen and The Stranger had moved out of the cottage. He wanted his little girl at home. Now he and Helen's mother were learning the manual alphabet. But Captain Keller wasn't trying very hard.

"What's the use?" he kept saying.

"You're going to need it," The Stranger told him. "Sooner or later—and I believe it will be before very long—Helen will know the meaning of words. And then you can talk to her, with your fingers in her hand."

Helen was now much quieter and better behaved than she had been. Everybody noticed it. She did not have so many tantrums. And when she did have one, it did not last long. But sometimes, as on this April morning, she would wake up feeling out of sorts and cross. For one thing, she was getting bored with the word game. "I know all that," she would think impatiently. "Why don't we play something else?"

All the morning The Stranger had been spelling two words into Helen's hand, W-A-T-E-R and C-U-P. She would spell C-U-P and give her a cup to hold. Then she would pour a little water into the cup, dip Helen's fingers into it, and wait hopefully for Helen to spell back W-A-T-E-R.

But Helen, not understanding, would spell C-U-P.

"What is it you want?" she kept thinking. "I'd do it if I knew. But I don't know. Can't you see I'm trying?"

"Poor child, you're getting tired," The Stranger said as Helen jerked her hand away and nearly upset the cup. "Let's rest awhile. Here!"

And she handed her the new doll she had brought her from Boston. Helen played with the doll awhile, but she was thinking of the word game.

"What do you want?" she kept saying to herself. "Why can't I do it? I try and try!"

Presently The Stranger started in on the word game again. C-U-P. W-A-T-E-R. But Helen kept getting more and more mixed up and irritable. Finally she seized her doll and dashed it to the floor. Its head broke in half a dozen pieces.

With grim satisfaction, she followed with her hands The Stranger's motions as she swept up the broken pieces.

"I don't care!" Helen told herself fiercely. "I don't care the least little bit! Why don't you leave me alone?"

She gave a little sigh of relief when The Stranger brought her hat to her. They were going outdoors. No more of that stupid game.

Although Helen did not know it, The Stranger carried the cup in her hand as they walked down the path toward the pump house.

Helen raised her head and sniffed with pleasure. That sweet smell! Although she didn't know the word for it, it was honeysuckle. She reached out her hand and touched the vine lovingly as they passed.

Someone was pumping water. The Stranger led Helen to the pump, placed the cup in her hand again, and held it under the spout.

Helen's first impulse was to throw the cup away. But she liked the sensation as the cool water flowed down over her hand into the cup. So she held it there, smiling a little.

The Stranger took hold of her other hand and began to spell the word again. W-A-T-E-R. Slowly at first. Then faster. Over and over again.

Suddenly Helen dropped the cup. She stood absolutely still, rigid, hardly breathing. Inside her mind, a new thought spun round and round:

" W-A-T-E-R! W-A-T-E-R! This lovely, cool stuff. W-AT-E-R!"

Wildly she groped for The Stranger's hand. Her trembling little fingers began, W-A-T—? She had not finished when she felt The Stranger's pat of approval on her shoulder. She was right!

That was it!

For the first time in her life, Helen Keller had "talked" with another human being!

The Stranger's eyes were wet as she cried: "Helen, you've got it! You've got it!"

Helen could not hear her. But that did not matter. For now another idea came flashing into her mind.

If that stuff was W-A-T-E-R, what about the other games they played with their hands?

She reached down and touched the ground, then turned eagerly to The Stranger. Her heart pounding like a little hammer, she felt The Stranger's fingers moving in her hand.

Several times The Stranger's fingers spelled the word, Helen intently following every movement. Then she spelled it back. G-R-O-UN-D. She had it fixed in her memory now. She would not forget.

Now she must find out about more things, fast! She ran about, touching everything she could reach. The Stranger's fingers told her

V-I-N-E, P-U-M-P, T-R-E-L-L-I-S. Helen bumped into the nurse, who was coming into the pump house carrying Helen's baby sister, Mildred, whom she still thought of as "It." She touched "It" and ran back to The Stranger, B-AB-Y! It had been spelled into her hand many, many times. Now it had meaning. Little Mildred was no longer just a thing called "It."

Suddenly Helen stood still, thinking hard. Then she reached out toward The Stranger.

Although she could not put it into words, as you or I would, her hand grasping The Stranger's hand asked a question:

"Who are you?"

And into her eager little palm the word came back: T-E-A-C-H-E-R.

In that warm, glowing moment all the hostility Helen had felt toward The Stranger melted away. For no longer was she a stranger. She was Teacher.

T-E-A-C-H-E-R! To Helen Keller, the most important word she would ever learn. And to Anne Sullivan, the most beautiful.

This passage may be used to practice the Extension Drill.

A. Add the total number of words on any three full lines of your book.	
B. Divide the total (A) by three to find the average words per line.	
C. Count the total number of lines that you read in one minute.	
D. Multiply the answers of B times C, or the average number of words per line times WPM the number of lines that you read.	WPM

EXAMPLE FROM "W-A-T-E-R":

A. Total number of words on three full lines	22
B. Divide A by three	7
C. Total number of lines read	31
D. Multiply B times C	217 WPM

A. Total number of words on three full lines	
B. Divide A by three	
C. Total number of lines read	
D. Multiply B times C	WPM

It is very important that you use your hand as a pacer for as much of your daily reading as possible. As with any habit, the more you practice, the quicker it becomes a useful, comfortable habit.

- Read at least one hour before Lesson Three, using your hand as a pacer. Read any book or magazine of your choice; it need not be done in one sitting.

- Practice the Extension Drill at least four times before going on to Lesson Three.

Extension Drill

1. From any beginning point, read for one minute. Mark your ending point. Compute your rate.

   Note: To time yourself, use a timer or set a watch with a sweep second hand near your book or magazine.

2. Reread the same material for one minute; read faster and farther. Mark your book or magazine.

3. Reread the same material for one minute; read even faster and farther. Mark your new ending point.

4. Reread the same material for one minute; read faster and even farther. Mark your new ending point.

5. In new material, read for one minute for good comprehension. Mark your ending point, and compute your rate.

Use the table on the next page to track your progress.

This is a weekly report of your progress at daily practice drills. With practice you will notice improvement in your reading rate from day to day and week to week. Make it your goal to attempt ever-increasing rates.

First Time	Time spent on drill: _____ mins.	Range of reading rates: _____ to _____ Low High	Comments:
Second Time	Time spent on drill: _____ mins.	Range of reading rates: _____ to _____ Low High	Comments:
Third Time	Time spent on drill: _____ mins.	Range of reading rates: _____ to _____ Low High	Comments:
Fourth Time	Time spent on drill: _____ mins.	Range of reading rates: _____ to _____ Low High	Comments:

Practice Summary

Record on your Progress Report Chart.

Total Time Spent on Drills: _____

Highest Reading Rate: _____

What You Need for This Lesson:

Evelyn Wood Course Guide

Audio CD #2

Pencil or pen

An easy novel or biography of your choice

Lesson 3

Double Your Reading Speed

Evelyn Wood
READING DYNAMICS®

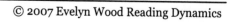

Practice using your hand as a pacer as much of the time as possible. Complete the following assignments before going on to Lesson Four:

- Read at least one hour before Lesson Four, using your hand as a pacer. This reading may be done in any book or magazine of your choice, and it need not be done all in one sitting.

- Practice the Push-Down Drill at least four times before going on to Lesson Four.

Push-Down Drill

1. From any beginning point, read for one minute. Mark your ending point, and compute your rate.

2. Reread the same material in 50 seconds. Strive to make your mark.

3. Reread the same material in 40 seconds, making your mark.

4. Practice read the same section in 30 seconds, making the mark.

5. Practice read the same section in 25 seconds, making the mark.

6. Practice read the same section in 20 seconds, making the mark.

7. From the end of the section that you've been practicing, read new material as fast as you can with good comprehension. You have one minute. Mark your ending point, and compute your rate.

Use the table on the next page to track your progress.

This is a weekly report of your progress at daily practice drills. With practice you will notice improvement in your reading rate from day to day and week to week. Make it your goal to attempt ever-increasing rates.

	Time spent on drill:	Range of reading rates:	Comments:
First Time	_____ mins.	_____ to _____ Low High	
Second Time	_____ mins.	_____ to _____ Low High	
Third Time	_____ mins.	_____ to _____ Low High	
Fourth Time	_____ mins.	_____ to _____ Low High	

Practice Summary

Record on your Progress Report Chart.

Total Time Spent on Drills: _____

Highest Reading Rate: _____

What You Need for This Lesson:

Evelyn Wood Course Guide

Audio CD #2

Pencil or pen

Blank paper, lined or unlined

A book of your choice, fiction or non-fiction

Lesson 4

*Remember More of What
You Read*

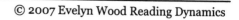

Directions: On the main diagonal line, answer the question, "What is it about?" On branch lines, add supporting items and details. Add branches if you need them.

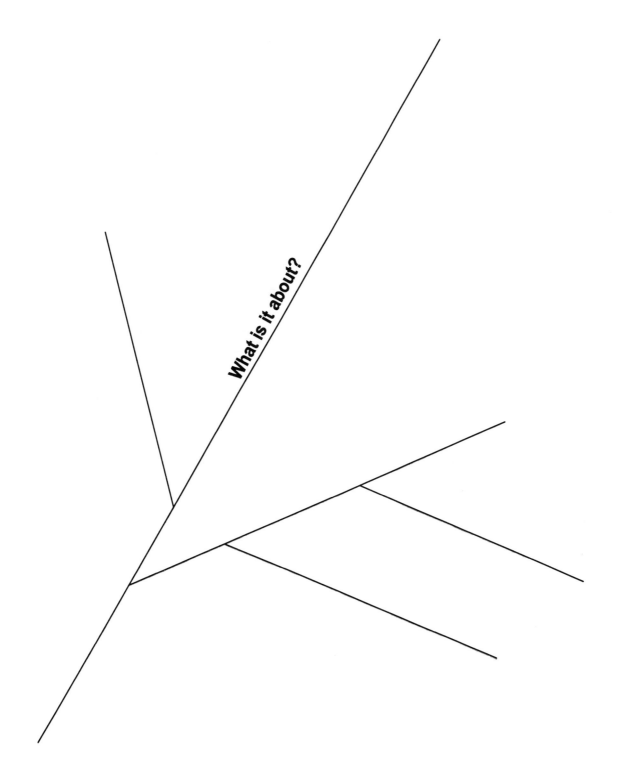

What is it about?

In addition to using your hand as a pacer for as much of your daily reading as possible, also make Slash Recall Patterns for as many readings as you can in order to develop the habit of immediate recall.

Complete the following assignments before going on to Lesson Five:

- Read at least one hour before Lesson Five, using your hand as a pacer. This reading may be done in any book of your choice, and it need not be done all at one sitting.

- Practice the Add Half a Page Drill at least four times before going on to Lesson Five.

Add Half a Page Drill

1. From any beginning point, read for one minute. Mark your ending point with a number 1, and compute your rate.

2. Put a number 2 one-half page ahead; go back to the same starting point above, and practice reading to the 2 in one minute. Be sure to make your mark.

3. Put a number 3 one-half page ahead; go back to the same starting point above, and practice reading to the 3 in one minute. Be sure to make the mark.

4. Put a number 4 one-half page ahead; practice reading this larger section in one minute, making your mark.

5. Put a number 5 one-half page ahead; practice reading this larger section in one minute, making the mark.

6. Go back to the number 1 in your book, and read as far as you can for good comprehension for one minute. Make an X mark where you stopped reading; make a Slash Recall Pattern; then go back and compute your rate.

Use the table on the next page to track your progress.

This is a weekly report of your progress at daily practice drills. With practice you will notice improvement in your reading rate from day to day and week to week. Make it your goal to attempt ever-increasing rates.

First Time	Time spent on drill: _____ mins.	Range of reading rates: _____ to _____ Low High	Comments:
Second Time	Time spent on drill: _____ mins.	Range of reading rates: _____ to _____ Low High	Comments:
Third Time	Time spent on drill: _____ mins.	Range of reading rates: _____ to _____ Low High	Comments:
Fourth Time	Time spent on drill: _____ mins.	Range of reading rates: _____ to _____ Low High	Comments:

Practice Summary

Record on your Progress Report Chart.

Total Time Spent on Drills: _____

Highest Reading Rate: _____

What You Need for This Lesson:

Evelyn Wood Course Guide

Audio CD #3

Pencil or pen

Blank paper

A book of your choice, fiction or non-fiction

Lesson 5

Push for Greater Reading Rates

Years ago when I was much younger and bolder, I was so frustrated by my own slow reading that I determined to teach myself to read faster and better, then try to teach high school students what I had learned to do for myself. I studied the reading authorities. I read their definitions of reading and found they could not agree how to define reading or comprehension so they made up their own definitions to fit their own needs. I studied the experiments of Cattell and Buswell and many others in the field. I became confused. The educational literature contains such references as: In the May 1950 issue of *Education,* Elizabeth Simpson is quoted as saying, "Of course, no one would assume that while the tachistoscopic studies show we can recognize a word at 1/100th of a second, it is also true we can read 6,000 words in a minute. We know we can't recognize so many ideas so quickly." I began to think—what if the 6,000 words represented only one or two ideas? Would this make a difference? It is in the field where we know things can't be done that so much is being done. Some authorities assured me reading must be done along the line, seeing most of the words; and that span is horizontal, making the idea situation two or three fixations along the line. Nila Banton Smith, in her book *Read Faster,* page 244, says, "We fixate at a point along the line and see all the words we can see to the left and right of the fixation, then move on to another fixation and repeat the perception process." Then she adds this observation: "But it happens that we also possess a vertical field of vision which usually lies dormant insofar as reading is concerned." I wondered why someone didn't do something to explore the potentialities of this field.

Use your hand as a pacer for all your daily reading.

Complete the following assignments before going on to Lesson Six:

- Read at least one hour before Lesson Six, using your hand as a pacer. This reading may be done in any book or magazine of your choice, and it need not be done all at one sitting.

- Do the Push-Up Drill at least four times before going on to the next lesson.

Push-Up Drill

1. Read from a beginning point for one minute for good comprehension. Mark your ending point, and compute your rate. Optional: Begin a Slash Recall Pattern.

2. Reread the same material for one minute; try to go farther. Make a new mark if you read farther ahead and erase the former one. Optional: Add to your Slash Recall Pattern.

3. Reread the same material again for one minute; go farther still. Make a new mark if you read farther ahead and erase the former one. Optional: Add to your Slash Recall Pattern.

4. Set up a second section of material immediately after and approximately equal to the amount covered in number 3. Practice read both sections in one minute. You must make the mark!

5. Set up a third section of material approximately equal to the section set up in number 4. Practice read all three sections in one minute. Make the mark!

6. Read new material for one minute for good comprehension. Make a mark where you stopped reading, and compute your rate. Optional: Add to your Slash Recall Pattern.

Use the table on the next page to track your progress

This is a weekly report of your progress at daily practice drills. With practice you will notice improvement in your reading rate from day to day and week to week. Make it your goal to attempt ever-increasing rates.

First Time	Time spent on drill: _____ mins.	Range of reading rates: _____ to _____ Low High	Comments:
Second Time	Time spent on drill: _____ mins.	Range of reading rates: _____ to _____ Low High	Comments:
Third Time	Time spent on drill: _____ mins.	Range of reading rates: _____ to _____ Low High	Comments:
Fourth Time	Time spent on drill: _____ mins.	Range of reading rates: _____ to _____ Low High	Comments:

Practice Summary

Record on your Progress Report Chart.

Total Time Spent on Drills: _____

Highest Reading Rate: _____

What You Need for This Lesson:

Evelyn Wood Course Guide

Audio CD #3

Pencil or pen

Blank paper

A newspaper of your choice (optional)

Lesson 6

Read the Newspaper More Efficiently

Proposed Budget Expected to Meet With Opposition

When Mayor Marc LaFrette presents his proposed budget to the City Council today, he isn't likely to be the most popular guy in town. LaFrette's budget will reverse a 10-year trend of reducing, or at least capping, property taxes.

Ten years ago, voters overwhelmingly approved a referendum requiring property tax revenue could not grow more than 3 percent a year.

In order to comply with the referendum, the tax rate would have to be reduced about a half mil, translating to about $24 million in revenue. This revenue is needed for city services such as police and fire protection. "It would be irresponsible to continue down this road of reducing revenue while our population is in such a growth phase," said Rose Blankenship, public relations director for the city.

So how will the mayor get around the referendum? A legal team of advisors argues that referendums are not legally binding.

But while he may win a legal battle, he may lose the popular opinion battle. "What's the point in voting for something if they can just ignore it!" argued Northside resident Rodney Grant.

The previous two mayors chose to stick with the referendum.

LaFrette campaigned heavily on making the government more efficient. Many opponents argue that LaFrette should focus on cutting unnecessary waste, rather than raising the tax revenue. "Raising taxes is the easy way out!" says Jeremy Blanchard, who opposed LaFrette in last year's election. "Anyone can raise taxes, but it takes a real leader to manage expenses while still providing a strong quality of life to residents."

While the budget will be presented today, the City Council is not expected to vote on it for two weeks.

The proposed budget will still have a reduction in the millage rate, but will only save the average household about $5 a year.

Historically, voters have not responded well to ignored referendums. Former Mayor Sandra Myers lost a reelection bid after a fierce battle with political newcomer James Stockton. Analysts suggest that Myers' changes to the school funding referendum cost her that election.

Holiday Cheer Hurts Job Seekers

In a season of shopping, packages, parties, and festivities, Chester Smith isn't feeling very jolly. Out of work since September, Smith says employment opportunities have dried up since the beginning of the holiday season.

"I was finding two or three jobs every week to apply for," Smith comments. "Since Thanksgiving, I'm lucky if I find even one a week."

Smith's experience isn't unusual. According to the Department of Labor, hiring activity is down across the country.

Analysts say it isn't a sign of a downturn in the economy, but rather a yearly cycle that is quite common. "We often see a dip in recruitment and hiring activity from mid-November through mid-January, "comments Janice Franssen of Franssen and Associates, a headhunting firm based in Charlotte.

According to Franssen, this period of inactivity is followed by one of the most active times of the year when hiring is at its peak from mid-January to mid-February. The January surge can be attributed to new funding available at the first of the year, and making up for lost time. "Employers are often scrambling to fill positions that they didn't have time to deal with over the holidays," according to Franssen.

This may not bring too much comfort to job seekers like Smith. "Two months is a long time to wait for the job market to pick up, especially when the kids are still expecting Christmas presents!"

The current unemployment rate is lower than this time last year, providing some hope to those still looking.

Employment is actually at its highest for the year in the retail, food service, and travel industries. "We're hiring people on the spot in some cases, "observes Francis McDonough, general manager at the Wine Reserve Restaurant and Event Center. "We are booked solid for the next four weeks and can use all the help we can get."

Economic indicators for next year's job growth are mixed. Early reports on consumer spending for the holiday season are positive, yet rising oil prices and interest rates are likely to keep growth from being too strong.

"But I'm still out there—I'm still trying," promises Smith with a smile.

Early Birds Get a Jump on Hurricane Preparation

With hurricane season just around the corner, it is a good time to take stock of just how prepared you are.

"The best time to prepare for a storm is now," advises Chip Johnson of the Emergency Planning Council. "By the time you see a storm on the news, you are already at a disadvantage."

Last year's hurricane season provided proof. Long lines at grocery stores and home improvement retailers were common sights throughout the state. With a little planning, that could have been avoided, says Johnson.

With another active season predicted, Johnson recommends the following steps to make sure you are prepared.

Check your disaster supply kit to make sure it is complete and current. Check expiration dates on food items and medicine that may have been sitting around for a few years. Look for items that have to be replenished after last year's storms. "And don't forget to think about the growth of your family," recommends Johnson. "Last year, I talked to several families who thought they were prepared because they had a box in the garage from several years ago. They hadn't taken their new baby into account and were in a sticky situation when they ran out of diapers in the middle of the storm."

Make insurance claims easier to process by creating a file with insurance policies, receipts for big ticket items, and photos or a video of the contents of your house. Keep all this information in a portable, waterproof container in case you are faced with flooding or evacuation.

Create an evacuation plan for your family. Know what flood zone you are in and what the recommended evacuation routes are best for your area. Make advanced arrangements with friends or relatives who live inland in case you need to get away. Be sure to think about family pets as well. "Finding a hotel, shelter, or friend that will take your two large dogs might make things difficult," warns Johnson. "A little planning in advance can alleviate that hassle."

Make a checklist and gather supplies to prepare your house for the storm. Because storms can change direction quickly, you may not have a lot of time to prepare your house. A checklist, assigned duties, and adequate supplies on hand can make the process smooth and quick.

"Fortunately, a hurricane is one of the most polite natural disasters," jokes Johnson. "You know they are coming and you usually have a few days notice." But if everyone is waiting to prepare in those few days, it can become a real nightmare. "That's why I like to prepare, so I can sit in my easy chair, ready for the storm, watching all the procrastinators on the news standing in line."

Use your hand as a pacer for all your daily reading.

Complete the following assignments before going on to Lesson Seven:

- Read at least one hour before Lesson Seven, using your hand as a pacer. This reading may be done in any book or magazine of your choice, and it need not be done all at one sitting.

- Do the Newspaper Reading Drill given below at least four times before going on to the next lesson.

- Optional: Do the Push-Up Drill from the last lesson four times before going on to Lesson Seven.

Newspaper Reading Drill

1. Look at only the headlines of the front page and any other favorite pages, such as the sports page or business page. If there is a summary of the day's news, read that.

2. Decide from step one what you wish to read in 10 minutes. If there is no news summary, then quickly thumb through the entire paper, just looking at headlines and deciding what you will read.

3. Beginning at the front page, read as quickly as you can just those articles you have decided to read. Read only as far in the article as you need to fulfill your purpose in reading it. Stop at the end of 10 minutes.

4. Roughly calculate how many pages you covered in 10 minutes. Each day try to cover more pages.

Use the table on the next page to track your progress.

This is a weekly report of your progress at daily practice drills. With practice you will notice improvement in your reading rate from day to day and week to week. Make it your goal to attempt ever-increasing rates.

	Time spent on drill:	Range of reading rates:	Comments:
First Time	_____ mins.	_____ to _____ Low High	
Second Time	_____ mins.	_____ to _____ Low High	
Third Time	_____ mins.	_____ to _____ Low High	
Fourth Time	_____ mins.	_____ to _____ Low High	

Practice Summary

Record on your Progress Report Chart.

Total Time Spent on Drills: _____

Highest Reading Rate: _____

What You Need for This Lesson:

Evelyn Wood Course Guide

Audio CD #4

Pencil or pen

Blank paper

A book of your choice, preferably a non-fiction book you haven't read or haven't read in a while.

Lesson 7

Develop Better Reading Comprehension

The Myth of the Overworked Executive

by Clarence B. Randall

A fine automobile is one of the miracles of modern engineering. Beneath the hood lies unlimited power, ready to lunge into immediate action at the slightest touch of the accelerator. Yet there is no unseemly outward manifestation of that power. Stand beside the car when the engine is running, and you scarcely hear a sound. There is no observable movement or vibration.

You cannot see the brakes, but they are wondrously efficient. The power can easily be released, but it can instantly be brought back under control. The car is always on the alert, always ready to do its job, but it is constructed for easy guidance and complete control at all times.

We have fine business executives who are like that. Their behavior is marked by outward calm and poise. Underneath lies tremendous personal capacity and power. Great effort is not signaled by outward commotion. They can take decisive action without breaking through the barriers of orderly restraint. In the African jungle, the lion roars as he springs for the kill, but among executives, those who are the leaders can exert their greatest strength without lifting their voices.

I am not, however, writing of these men, but of their opposites.

In nearly every organization, there is a self-appointed overworked executive. All day, every day, he advertises his martyrdom. His, he believes, is the pivotal responsibility in his company. Constantly sorry for himself because of the enormous burden he bears, he calls all men to witness the sacrifices he makes for the good of the company, sacrifices so little appreciated by his superior officers. Privately and yet to all who will listen, he pours out his personal woe, which is that he is badly underpaid.

Here is how you will know him: His desk is a mess. Papers are strewn across it in wild disarray, creating the impression that every important corporate transaction comes to him for approval. Yet, if you should discreetly make a few spotchecks, you would find that many of the letters and memos that he paws through to find the one you are after were there last week. They will be there next week, too. Should you find one day, to your surprise, a slight improvement, you would probably later discover that he achieved this in desperation by sweeping an armful of papers into the desk drawer.

Close by our hero's elbow is a large ashtray, half full of partly smoked cigarettes, to indicate the extreme nervous tension under which he operates.

He seldom goes out to lunch, but has a sandwich and a glass of milk brought in. This adds to the buildup. Not a moment of his time must be lost, or earnings for the month will go off sharply.

In his hand when he leaves the office is the inevitable bulging briefcase. He would no more be caught without that mark of martyrdom than he would be seen without his trousers. True, many of the papers in it have already made a great many round trips without being disturbed. But, nevertheless, this nightly show makes it clear to all that here is a very important man.

When finally he bursts in the front door of his house, he pecks his wife hastily on the cheek and expects to sit down at the table immediately. He must never be kept waiting. He has dropped his briefcase in the front hall, where it is likely to stay till morning if there should happen to be a night ball game on. At best it will be a tug-of-war between the papers and the blare of television for several hours.

There will be little general family conversation.

One of this man's proudest boasts is that he has not had a vacation in 10 years. "Just can't take the time," he says. That his wife deserves one, and that his family is growing up without the joy of experiences shared with him, are considerations outside his realm of understanding. Actually, his capacity for enjoyment is so atrophied that he would not know what to do with a vacation if forced into it. Nonetheless, he will soon have one involuntarily—in a hospital—when his coronary thrombosis comes, as it surely will.

He is greatly given to travel, rushing about on planes, briefcase in hand, as though the number of miles flown in a year were any criterion of effective effort. Physical activity gives him a proud sense of doing. Often a long distance call, if prudently planned and intelligently carried through, would fully answer the purpose; but that would somehow downgrade the whole transaction. Nor does he ever achieve much by correspondence, since he has never learned to express himself cogently and persuasively in a letter.

What little responsibility he bears he shares with no one. To simplify his day by delegating to juniors the routine clerical part of his tasks would deflate his ego. Neither superior officer nor associate is ever quite sure just what it is that occupies him so intensively. If something takes him away from his desk, whether for an hour or for a week, everything stops.

Partly this is because it gives him satisfaction to surround himself with a slight air of mystery. For example, he is highly secretive about his personal affairs. He would not think of letting a secretary handle his checkbook or take his deposits to the bank. She might find out how small his income really is in comparison with the image he is endeavoring to create.

He has never had a will drawn, has never had a frank talk with his wife as to what to do or whom to consult in case of his death, or told her what she may expect by way of income during her remaining years. His meager insurance policies are not collected in one place, and his social security card is long since lost.

He is chronically late for all engagements. When a staff conference is called, he bustles into the room 15 minutes after it has been begun, wearing an air of preoccupation that is intended to suggest to his colleagues that it is generous indeed for a man who bears such manifest responsibility to take time for such lesser matters at all.

In his office he keeps visitors waiting beyond the time set for the engagement, partly because his awareness of his surroundings is so low that he is actually not conscious of the passage of time, and partly because by delaying others he reminds himself once more of his own importance.

The presence of such a disordered life within an organization can have repercussions that are the very antithesis of good management. Inevitably, this man becomes a focal point from which confusion and uncertainty spread. Policy is neither reliably implemented by such an individual nor accurately transmitted to others. Because he cannot discipline himself, he can neither lead nor discipline others.

The fault lies within. What is missing is the inner poise and deep humility that come from the continuous development of the adult mind and spirit.

A person of this type is almost invariably one who early abandoned the cultivation of the mind. Yet, sadly enough, he is more often than not a college graduate. He has no intellectual satisfactions. From one year's end to the next, he never enters into the companionship of great minds by good reading. He confines himself strictly to the daily paper, principally the financial and sporting sections, and to his trade journals. He hears no concerts, attends no art exhibits, participates in no discussion groups. He has no views on the questions of the day other than a continuing stream of verbose invective directed toward all those in authority.

In the realm of the spirit, he possesses no basic philosophy to which he may turn in times of stress. He has no sense of values that find expression in his life from day to day, values that others come to recognize and respect. Yet mental serenity and internal resources are never lacking in the truly great executives of American industry. They must, of course, have fine minds and strong wills. But the power of their personalities finds expression through order and a self discipline so immaculate that it is seldom apparent as a separable trait of character.

When a visitor is shown in to a good executive, he finds before him a clean desk and behind it a man who is at ease, who makes him feel that this is the call he has been waiting for, and who listens attentively. Yet, subtly, the man behind the desk is in control of the interview all of the time and knows how to terminate it without giving offense.

The good executive also has a plan for his day. He knows what things have to be accomplished if the required tempo is to be maintained, and times himself accordingly. With deliberate speed he moves from one task to the next, making his decisions resolutely when he senses the matter has consumed the maximum period that can be allotted to it. There is no outward sign of inner struggle, and the job gets done.

He works a full day, though not an overly long one. When the normal quitting time comes, except for those sudden emergencies that no man can control, he will walk promptly out of office with a sense of satisfaction at what he has accomplished. And in closing the door, he will put it all behind him. His evenings and his weekends bring him a change of pace. In company with his family and neighbors, he turns with high enthusiasm to other challenging interests that are totally unrelated to his daily routines. When he comes back to his job, both his body and his mind have been refreshed.

His ideas do not become inbred, because he spends a great deal of time with people who know nothing whatever about his business and who are not particularly impressed with his responsibilities. Many of them do not even know what he does, and care less. This helps him keep his own importance in perspective.

He has a zest for vacations. He knows that rotation of interests is as important to the productivity of the mind as rotation of crops is to the fertility of the soil.

He has the excellent characteristic of laughing well. His lively and infectious sense of humor lubricates all of his human relationships.

In short, the self-pitying, overworked executive is a man who presses badly. The fine executive is one who always takes a free, easy swing at the ball.

Use your hand as a pacer for all your daily reading. Do the following assignments before going on to Lesson Eight:

- Read at least one hour before Lesson Eight, using your hand as a pacer. This reading may be done in any book or magazine of your choice.

- Do the Dynamic Reading Drill employing the Multiple Reading Process, given below, at least four times before going on to the next lesson.

Dynamic Reading Drill

1. Select a chapter of about 10 pages (300 to 500 words per page) from an interesting book, preferably non-fiction.

2. Using the techniques learned in this lesson, preview the chapter as fast as you can—one to two minutes should be plenty of time. Find what the important points of the chapter are, so you can decide your reading purpose.

3. Read the chapter as fast as you can, keeping your purpose in mind. Speed up where comprehension comes easily; slow down where it is more difficult. Calculate your rate.

4. Decide if there is anything that you seem to be missing from the material, anything that you wish to clarify or check or just go over again. Then postview the section in one to two minutes with the goal of getting that information.

To compute a rate while reading a whole chapter:

A. Keep track of the total time used (in quarters of minutes): _____

B. Compute the average words per page (rounded off): _____

C. Multiply the words per page by the number of pages read: _____

This is a weekly report of your progress at daily practice drills. With practice you will notice improvement in your reading rate from day to day and week to week. Make it your goal to attempt ever-increasing rates.

	Time spent on drill:	Range of reading rates:	Comments:
First Time	_____ mins.	_____ to _____ Low High	
Second Time	_____ mins.	_____ to _____ Low High	
Third Time	_____ mins.	_____ to _____ Low High	
Fourth Time	_____ mins.	_____ to _____ Low High	

Practice Summary

Record on your Progress Report Chart.

Total Time Spent on Drills: _____

Highest Reading Rate: _____

What You Need for This Lesson:

Evelyn Wood Course Guide

Audio CD #4

Pencil or pen

Blank paper

A non-fiction book of your choice

Lesson 8

Organize What You've Read to Remember It

Evelyn Wood
READING DYNAMICS®

apples
dry cereal
sugar
pork chops
milk
butter
eggs
steak
toilet paper
glass
cleaner
bread
rice
peas

broccoli
chicken
macaroni
cheese
potatoes
green beans
lettuce
tomatoes
soft drinks
cucumbers
ice cream
carrots
shrimp
sour cream

flour
coffee
paper
towels
spare ribs
spinach
hamburger
bacon
jam
cheesecake
beer
paper
napkins
cupcakes

tuna fish
cold cuts
cottage
cheese
steel wool
laundry

When the items are organized into groups of seven items or fewer, they are easier to remember than 46 single items.

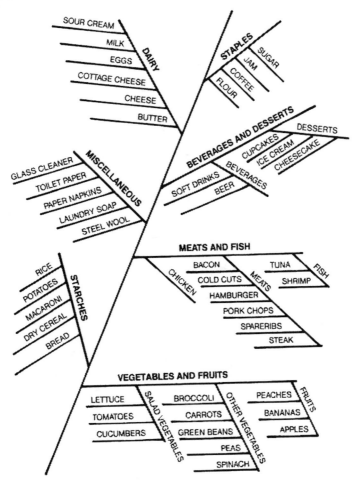

Psychology Today

"Stages of Development"

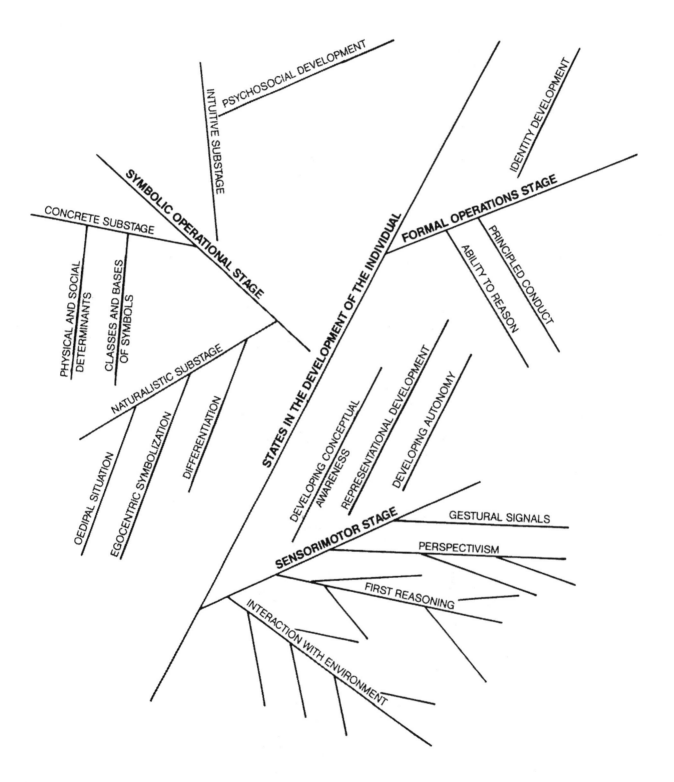

The Old Man and the Sea
by Ernest Hemingway

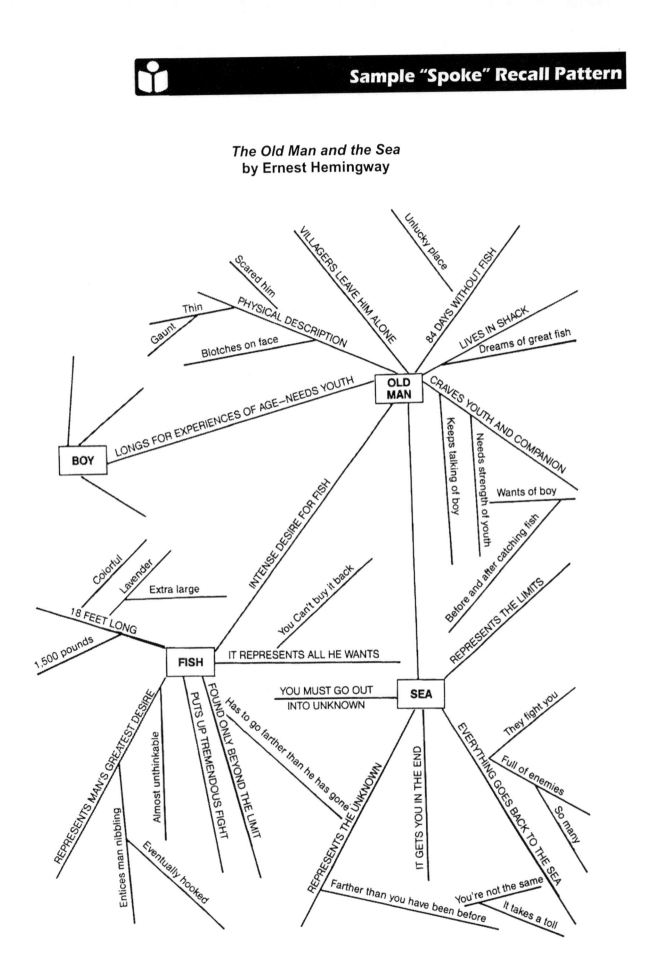

Legal Problems in Engineering

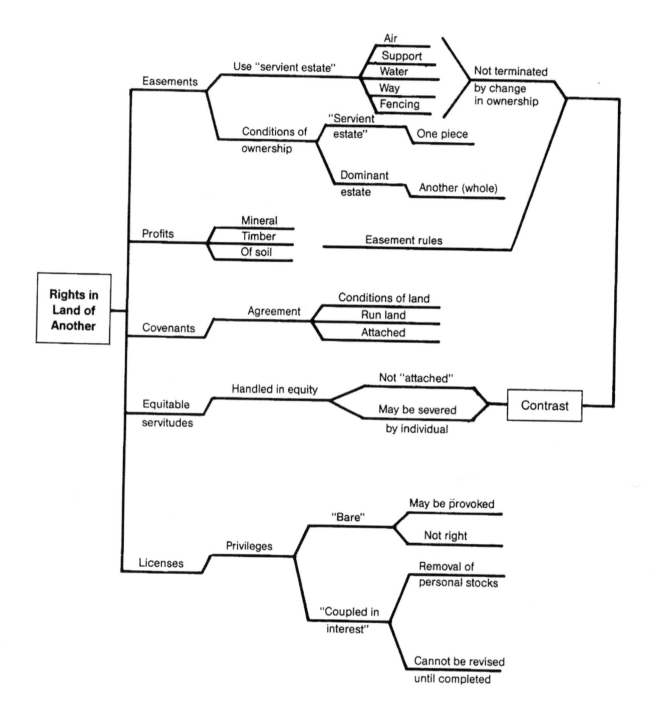

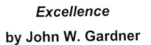

Excellence

by John W. Gardner

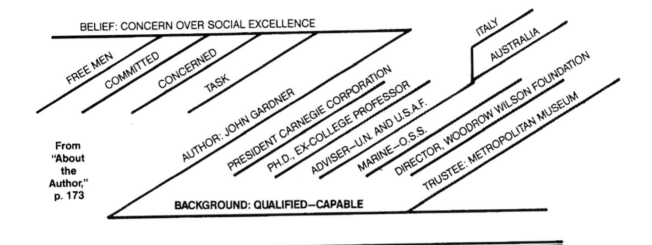

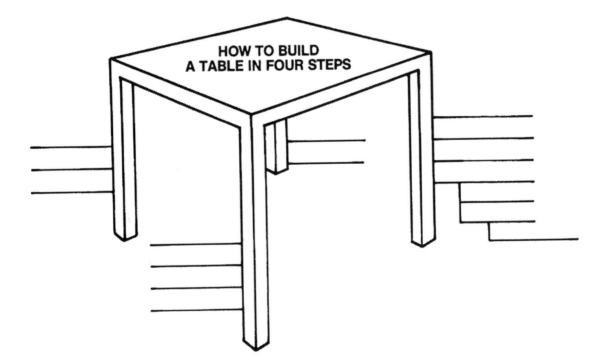

1. *Be selective when you read.*

2. *Develop a point of view toward the material; grasp its structure or theme.*

3. *Read with a definite purpose to satisfy an interest.*

4. *Organize as you read.*

5. *After reading, do something creative and useful with the information.*

Use your hand as a pacer for all your daily reading. Do the following assignments before you begin Lesson Nine:

- Read at least one hour before Lesson Nine, using your hand as a pacer. This reading may be done in any book or magazine of your choice, and it need not be done all at one sitting.

- Practice the Dynamic Reading Drill given below, using the Multiple Reading Process, at least four times before going on to the next lesson.

Dynamic Reading Drill

1. Select a chapter of approximately 10 pages from an interesting book of non-fiction.

2. Scan the whole chapter to locate subheads and any other signs of the author's organization of the material. Set up a Recall Pattern to reflect the organization.

3. Preview the chapter for its main ideas. Stop and add to your Recall Pattern as much of the preview in formation as you can remember.

4. Read the chapter as fast as you can. Stop and add to your Recall Pattern any additional in formation you can remember. Calculate your reading rate for the entire reading.

5. Post-view the chapter as fast as you can. Stop and add new information to your slash Recall Pattern.

Use the table on the next page to track your progress.

This is a weekly report of your progress at daily practice drills. With practice you will notice improvement in your reading rate from day to day and week to week. Make it your goal to attempt ever-increasing rates.

	Time spent on drill:	Range of reading rates:	Comments:
First Time	_____ mins.	_____ to _____ Low High	
Second Time	_____ mins.	_____ to _____ Low High	
Third Time	_____ mins.	_____ to _____ Low High	
Fourth Time	_____ mins.	_____ to _____ Low High	

Practice Summary

Record on your Progress Report Chart.

Total Time Spent on Drills: _____

Highest Reading Rate: _____

What You Need for This Lesson:

Evelyn Wood Course Guide

Audio CD #5

Pencil or pen

Blank paper

A textbook or non-fiction book of your choice

Lesson 9

Develop Dynamic Study Skills

For the book as a whole:	
Conduct an Overview	Overview the jacket or cover of the book, and read about the author and any other information. Examine the table of contents to understand the organization of the book.

For each chapter, analyze the whole:	
Overview	Inspect style, form, organization, and look over any maps, photos, illustrations, footnotes, etc.
Set Your Purpose	Use summaries and questions at the end to decide what you need from the material. What may be gained? What is essential?
Preview and Divide	Look over the whole, isolating where the necessary information lies, and divide the whole into manageable sections, according to your purpose.
Recall and Question	Set up a recall format with a place for each section. Create questions for each section.

For each section:	
Preview and Recall	Preview for main ideas only. In some cases, it will be necessary to first write down dates and other essentially structural information.
Read and Recall	Read for additional in formation to fill in main ideas. Check difficult areas that will require rereading or clarifying.

Reorganize the whole:	
Reorganize	Read checked material. Repeat until your purpose is met (until you can recall in your own words the necessary information).
Remember and Review	Reorganize the recall pattern; develop your own relationships and organization (book closed); do it in a new way. To review, reconstruct Recall Patterns from memory at regular intervals.

This Slash Recall Pattern is set up using the author's organization. This chapter is broken into three main parts (represented by the three main branches) and each part has as many sections as there are subbranches. Some sections have subsections. After this is completed, take each section or subsection to preview and recall, then read and recall, until your purpose is met—when you recall enough without looking at the material to feel that you really know it.

Psychology Today

"Stages of Development"

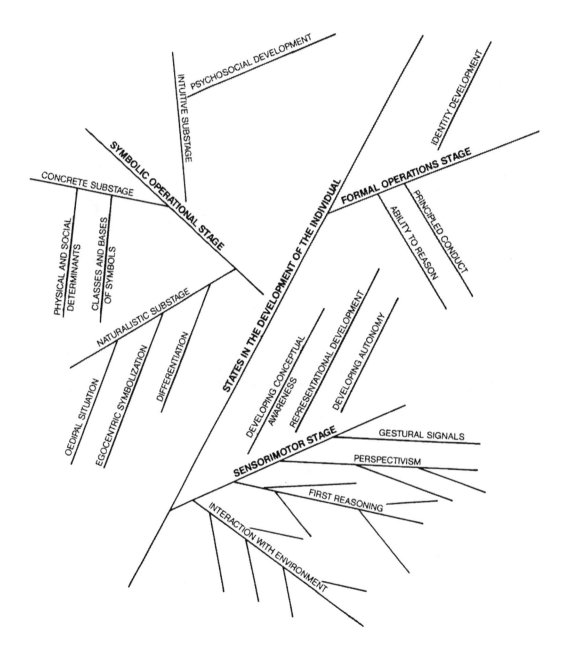

by Claude Buss

Since 1949, China should be taken to mean the giant, complex nation-state in East Asia with the greatest population and the oldest continuing civilization in the world. Officially, China is called the People's Republic of China. It is the largest Communist country in the world.

The Land. Whatever China is called, it is larger than the United States, extending 2,000 miles from the north to the semitropical south; and nearly as great a distance from the China Seas on the east to the mountains and arid deserts of Central Asia on the west.

The geographic panorama is too varied for general description; each locality and each season is special. China possesses tremendous urban centers like Beijing, its capital, and Shanghai, Canton, Hankow, Tientsin, Harbin and Mukden. It also has many smaller urban areas with populations of more than 100,000 inhabitants, and a host of towns which we might regard as county seats.

The People. China's overall population is over 1.3 billion—the largest in the world. The majority of China's people still live in clusters of homes or villages and make their livelihood from agriculture.

The Culture. The Chinese have a sense of oneness which stems from their written language, common way of life, and Confucian tradition. Confucius was a contemporary of Socrates. His thought and philosophy, as interpreted by generations of disciples, have influenced the Chinese as much as the combined writings of the Greek philosophers and Christian theologians have shaped the intellectual life of the West.

An inextinguishable love of life and persistent sense of beauty have created a vital artistic tradition, while a high regard for the written word has given China a voluminous body of source materials. The country has been pursuing massive education programs, and there is a high degree of interest in all forms of literature.

Influence of the West. Along with its cultural tradition, China has inherited much of the political thought of the West. In the 19th century, the native way of life was shattered by the intrusion of Western merchants, missionaries, soldiers, and diplomats. Imperialism begat anti-imperialism and anti-imperialism begat revolution.

The Opium War of 1840 caused scarcely a stir in most of China, but the frightful T'ai P'ing rebellion (1854-1865) brought death to millions and spread destruction through a dozen provinces. Chinese conservatives were impotent to preserve the old order against the onslaught of new and modern ideas.

After China's defeat at the hands of Japan in 1894, China's great revolutionary, Sun Yat-sen, tried to rally his country against the decadent Manchu dynasty. His ideas gained immense support when, as a consequence of the Boxer Rebellion in 1900, a handful of foreign forces drove the imperial court out of the capital city. For the next decade, the Empress Dowager frantically tried to check the coming storm by building a new army and modernizing the political system. Her efforts were in vain. A revolution, which the Chinese now refer to as liberal democratic bourgeois revolution, broke out in 1911, and a Chinese republic replaced the ancient empire.

The republic, and the entire concept of popular government, got off to an unfortunate start in China. Those who espoused it were incompetent men. Civil authority gave way to warlords, and the poor suffered more than ever. Ideas of nationalism, democracy and social welfare grew in the minds of leaders sincerely desirous of putting an end to chaos. Sun Yat-sen led the Kuomintang party to victory and ostensible unification.

In the meantime, socialist and communist ideas began to proliferate. The Chinese Communists see the May 4, 1919, movement as the point at which the old revolution ended and the new one began. In 1921 a few Chinese intellectuals organized the Communist party of China and began their spectacular march to power. In 1949 this revolution culminated with the unification of all of China with the exception of Taiwan, the large island off the Chinese coast.

The Chinese Communists have thus received a double heritage: first, the ancient and humane culture of China; and second, the ideology of world communism. The combination of these two aspects, along with its profound nationalism, doubtless accounts for China's achievements since 1949. It should also help in the understanding of China's problems.

Their Achievements. It is idle to underestimate what the Chinese Communists have been able to accomplish. They have unified the country as it has never been before, and they have raised the overall standard of living. They have set into operation a centralized government that has shaped an undisciplined people into a gigantic tool of a dedicated party and in the process generated true nationalism.

Whatever the statistics, China has increased its agricultural production and has taken giant strides in industrialization.

Their Problems. The recognition of their achievements should be matched with an understanding of their problems. How can they maintain the momentum of their growth with the reality of the size and nature of their population? With the margin of subsistence already so slim, how can enough food be provided for so many additional stomachs each year?

China is faced with the enormous cost of its crash program in industrialization, as well as the cost of its administration and military. It also faces the cost and the national effort required to maintain its dominance in Asia and its influence throughout the world.

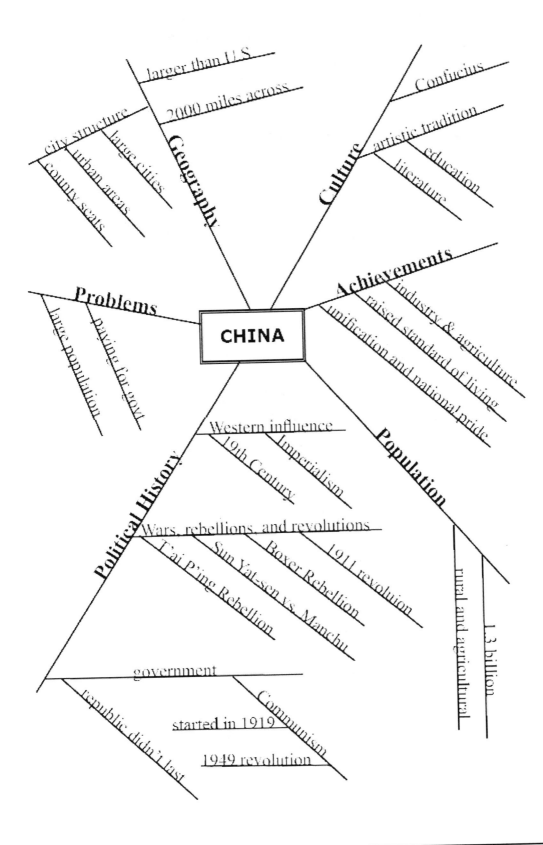

Geography
- larger than U.S.
- 2000 miles across
- city structure
- large cities
- urban areas
- county seats

Culture
- Confucius
- artistic tradition
- literature
- education

Achievements
- industry & agriculture
- raised standard of living
- unification and national pride

CHINA

Problems
- large population
- paying for govt.

Population
- rural and agricultural
- 1.3 billion

Political History
- Western influence
- 19th Century
- Imperialism
- Wars, rebellions, and revolutions
- 1911 revolution
- Boxer Rebellion
- Sun Yat-sen vs. Manchu
- T'ai Ping Rebellion
- government
- started in 1919
- Communism
- 1949 revolution
- republic didn't last

Test yourself: After studying the lesson on China, apply the study method. Take this quiz to determine how much you learned. Answers are located within the text. Answer the quiz based on what is in the text, not from other sources or personal opinion.

(It's good to occasionally practice study skills with older materials like this so that you must focus on the information in the passage rather than your current knowledge.)

1. Compare China and the United States in terms of "The Land" and "The People."

_____

_____

_____

_____

2. Describe one important aspect of the Chinese cultural heritage.

_____

3. List two items or incidents of Western influence on modern China.

_____

_____

4. Name two major achievements of the Chinese government.

_____

_____

5. Name one major problem that modern China faces.

_____

_____

Use your hand as a pacer for your daily reading. Complete the following supplemental practice before beginning Lesson Ten:

Read at least one hour before Lesson Ten, using your hand as a pacer. This reading may be done in any book or magazine of your choice.

- Practice the Study and Depth Reading Drill below at least four times before going on to the next lesson.

- Optional: Practice the Push-Down Drill four times before going on to Lesson Ten.

Study and Depth Reading Drill

If you are not a student, do not feel compelled to study a textbook. Select any informational book on a subject that interests you.

1. Select a chapter or section (it may be very short) in a textbook or a book of non-fiction that represents the most difficult reading you do. (Avoid math or science books that are mainly formulas and problems.)

2. Determine your reading purpose: to know it very thoroughly in order to pass a detailed test; to know it fairly well (to back up main ideas or theories with supporting facts); to become familiar with the main ideas; or to know the thesis of the chapter or section.

3. With your purpose decided, apply the study techniques. Adapt the techniques to meet your purpose.

Use the table on the next page to track your progress.

This is a weekly report of your progress at daily practice drills. With practice you will notice improvement in your reading rate from day to day and week to week. Make it your goal to attempt ever-increasing rates.

	Time spent on drill:	Range of reading rates:	Comments:
First Time	_____ mins.	_____ to _____ Low High	
Second Time	_____ mins.	_____ to _____ Low High	
Third Time	_____ mins.	_____ to _____ Low High	
Fourth Time	_____ mins.	_____ to _____ Low High	

Practice Summary

Record on your Progress Report Chart.

Total Time Spent on Drills: _____

Highest Reading Rate: _____

What You Need for This Lesson:

Evelyn Wood Course Guide

Audio CD #5

Pencil or pen

A book and a magazine of your choice

Optional: An electronic document, at least 4 pages long

Lesson 10

Breeze Through E-Mail, Letters and Magazines

Use your hand as a pacer for all your daily reading. Practice the following assignments before going on to Lesson Eleven:

- Read at least one hour before Lesson Eleven, using your hand as a pacer. This reading may be done in any book of your choice.

- Practice the Magazine Reading Drill given below at least four times before going on to the next lesson.

- Optional: Practice the Add Half a Page Drill four times before going on to the next lesson.

Magazine Reading Drill

1. Select a magazine to read, and overview the table of contents. Check with a pencil the articles that you most want to read, and assign priorities in their order of importance to you. (If there is no table of contents or if it does not give enough information, then quickly—in five minutes—thumb through the magazine, deciding what you want to read and assigning the priorities as you go.)

2. In 15 minutes, cover the whole magazine, reading one or two articles of the highest priority and previewing all others that you feel are important. See how much you can cover each day; you should be able to cover more and more material each time you do this drill. Estimate and record the amount of material covered in 15 minutes.

Use the table on the next page to track your progress.

This is a weekly report of your progress at daily practice drills. With practice you will notice improvement in your reading rate from day to day and week to week. Make it your goal to attempt ever-increasing rates.

First Time	Time spent on drill: _____ mins.	Range of reading rates: _____ to _____ Low High	Comments:
Second Time	Time spent on drill: _____ mins.	Range of reading rates: _____ to _____ Low High	Comments:
Third Time	Time spent on drill: _____ mins.	Range of reading rates: _____ to _____ Low High	Comments:
Fourth Time	Time spent on drill: _____ mins.	Range of reading rates: _____ to _____ Low High	Comments:

Practice Summary

Record on your Progress Report Chart.

Total Time Spent on Drills: _____

Highest Reading Rate: _____

What You Need for This Lesson:

Evelyn Wood Course Guide

Audio CD #6

Pencil or pen

Blank paper

A book of your choice

Lesson 11

Achieve Flexibility in Reading

Evelyn Wood
READING DYNAMICS®

1. Linear Read   2. Skim   3. Scan   4. Study Method

866-5931 Wright Richard 102EastAv
838-7641 Wright William J 15CheleneRd
838-6135 Wrigley Mildred E SLedgeRdRwytn
866-7994 Wrinn J J rl est 1 SGlenwoodAvSN
866-1322 Wu George 1-Oakfi eldRdSN
866-6080 -Boys Telephone
866-7881 WuhrerAnde 7-SeasidePIEN
866-1311 WuhrerSam 7-SeasidePIEN
847-9458 Wultf Frank R 195WRocksRd
846-2143 Wuskie Susan 32EastAv
847-0082 Wyman Lewis C 31 Noah'sLa
847-7770 Wynkoop John R Jr 134PerryAv
866-8337 Wynn Edward 29BurrittAvSN

X

─────── **XEROX CORPORATION**───────

STMFRD -Sales
329-881 1011HighRidgeRdStamford
853-1333 Fairfi eld County Technical
Service 445HamiltonAv
853-8001 XEXEX INDUSTRIES INC.
SDukePISN

Y

866-4425 Y M C A 370WestAv
853-2555 Yacht Queen Ann II BeachRdEN
853-4838 Yacht Rita-JCalfPastureBeachRdE
866-6400 Yacht Yankee Girl MackSN
838-0935 Yackulics John J CloverlyCircleEN
866-9003 Yackuiics Mary Mrs 7LocustEN
838-2485 Yager Bertha Mrs
846-1932 Yates Paul 164ERocksRd
853-6860 Yates Walter E 20NTaylorAvSN
838-7405 Yavne Israel Rabbi King
846-3130 Yavne Israel Rabbi 41WolfpitAv
847-9356 Yearout Floyd SilvermineAv
838-2476 Yerinides Gus 29-SummittAvSn
866-9124 Yerinides Joseph 1 SBayviewAvSN
846-
1329 YerkesACraig SAndersenRD
847-3393 Yff Robert SWildwoodLa
838-5005 Yobbagy Arthur 6LincolnAvSoN
838-2288 Yobbagy William 31PhillipsSoN
853-6627 Yoel M H 1 RollingLa
847-0894 Yoppe William J 199PonusAv
838-7802 Yordon Henry K Rev 9William
847-8487 York Glenn P 38-SilvermineAv
847-1603 Yorzinski Alexander 9Girard
853-0837 Yost Charles 11 Elm
846-1744 Yost Edmund W Jr 55NewtownAv

847-4853 Yost Elwood 20GlenAv
847-0265 Yost Harry CamelotDr
838-3235 Youhas Anthony Colony
846-9682 Young Brian 41WolfpitAv
846-1456 YOUNG DECORATORS 554MainAv
846-1594 Young Donald M 24DouglasDr
866-3924 Young Grace J Mrs 14ElmcrestTer
838-5874 Young Harry M 2HawkinsAvEN
866-8752 Young Ivory Sr MontereyPISN
846-0198 Yuan Kien 21DonohueDr
866-9823 Yunckes Gustav 1-OrlandoRd
866-6956 Yuscak Hazel 22FourthEN

Z

866-1612 Zabelle Realty rl est 104EastAv
836-0050 Zabelle Sidney 6RebelLa
866-6689 Zabelle Travel Agency 104EastAv
846-0200 Zabelle William 45Maple
866-0023 Zacarola John J 9EagleRd
838-8024 Zacc Bill 11 BluffAvRwtyn
854-9614 Zach Philip 40 5 Av
866-4939 Zack William J 14AlrowoodDr
847-4426 Zahlman Gaylord 31 DryHlRd
847-4794 Zahlman Velma Mrs 17BrtittMnr
838-8227 Zaino James V 48BaxterDrSn
838-6352 Zaino John 42-summittAvSN
847-3494 Zaino Patsy SBurlingtonCt
846-9274 Zakar Isidore 48Aiken
866-7112 ZakharAntone 22VanZantEN
866-7753 Zakhar George J 6RolandAvEN
838-9117 Zakhar James 48FifthEN
838-8228 Zakhar Joseph 76GrandviewAv
846-1258 Zakhar Robert SThames
846-9292 Zakhar William J 14HideawayLa
846-1065 Zaleski Frank 26-SurreyDr
847-8606 Zaleski Julius E Sr 20EIIS
866-4977 Zambrana Maria 55BoutonSN
838-4361 Zamm Edward J atty 222Main
847-9092 -Res AppletreeLa
838-4066 Zamm Pauline 26MonroeSn
847-2211 Zander Arthur H 21LancasterDr
866-5503 Zanesky Robert atty 110Wall WESTPT
847-8625 Zangrillo Robert InwoodRd
846-9601 ZannellaC 456NewtownAv
846-1702 Zannella Joseph 456NewtownAv

Time Used to Meet Purpose _____

1. Linear Read   2. Skim   3. Scan   4. Study Method

Internal Affairs

During the first four years under the constitution, 1954-1958, internal affairs were given priority. The Communists felt obliged to perfect their collective leadership, keep the armed forces at top strength, wrestle with minority problems, do something about Taiwan, maintain "purity" in the party and tighten the processes of thought control. The economic crises came after 1958.

Collective Leadership. Nowhere in the world during those years was there a more impressive leadership than in China. The party and the government worked at every level through interlocking directorates. In towns and villages, the people voted for representatives in local congresses and councils, who received orders telling them what to do from the general secretariat in Beijing. At the national level, the party hierarchy dominated the government and on occasion used an advisory body called the Supreme State Conference as a forum for important pronouncements. It converted the National Defense Council into a mere front for military direction.

Time Used to Meet Purpose: _____

1. Linear Read   2. Skim   3. Scan   4. Study Method

COUNTY BANK & TRUST COMPANY

808 MAIN STREET, DEERFIELD, IL 60015

January 12, 2006

Dear Mr. Pettingill:

It has been brought to my attention that you are three months behind in the payment of your loan #5876-43. We have received no replies to our several notices, nor have you returned our telephone calls.

Your loan was taken out to finance the cost of your daughter's college education. From personal experience, I understand how difficult it is to pay for our children's education. The bank can be quite understanding in matters of this nature, including offering financial planning support.

As of January 20, you will be four months behind. It is imperative that you immediately call to set up an appointment with me or one of the other officers. If we don't hear from you by the due date, procedures to rectify the situation will have to be taken. This could cause unnecessary embarrassment to you and your family. We would like to avoid this at all costs, but if we do not hear from you within one week, we have no other choice.

Sincerely,

Ann B. Long

Treasurer

Time Used to Meet Purpose: _____

1. Linear Read   2. Skim   3. Scan   4. Study Method

Police Officers May Be Eliminated

Police Commissioner David F. Crawford stated yesterday that height requirements might be eliminated for police officers.

Crawford said new qualifying tests were being considered that would do away with requirements that were not "job related" and might eliminate traditional height and athletic prowess requirements.

Candidates will be evaluated with new testing methods during their six-month training.

"Obviously, if a recruit is too small to sit behind the wheel of a police car or lacks some other necessary requirement, he or she could not become a police officer," Crawford added.

Current requirements for police officers have long been criticized by the minority community for keeping minority group applicants out for reasons unrelated to the job.

Davis Center Adds Dancing to Cultural Life

23-year-old Sara Teske performed the exotic art of the belly dance for 100 visitors to the Davis Center for Cultural Enrichment yesterday.

After her 15-minute performance, Teske, a newspaper editor in Greenville, taught basic belly dance movements to seven volunteers, ranging in age from 6 to 60.

"It was just great," exclaimed 25-year-old Maria Mendes of Oak Hills. "Even though I couldn't shake everything the way she did!"

Mendes said she summoned enough nerve to go on stage only after her parents had left the audience.

The instruction, which lasted about 15 minutes, allowed Edna Bauer of Lincoln Springs to brush up on the steps she learned several years ago. "It was a great dance down memory lane!"

Time Used to Meet Purpose: _____

Use your hand as a pacer for all your daily reading. Complete the following assignments before going on to Lesson Twelve:

- Read at least one hour before completing Lesson Twelve, using your hand as a pacer. This reading may be done in any book or magazine of your choice, and it need not be done all at one sitting.

- Practice the Overlap Drill on the next page at least four times before going on to the next lesson.

- Optional: Before beginning Lesson Twelve, review and practice each of the drills from the following lessons: Lessons Three, Four, Five and Seven.

Overlap Drill

1. From any starting point, read for good comprehension as fast as you can for one minute. Write the number "1" where you stop reading.

2. Read on in the new material for another minute. Write the number "2" where you stop reading. Optional: Create a Recall Pattern with information from Sections 1 and 2.

3. Practice read both Sections 1 and 2 in one minute, and be sure to make the mark.

4. Read on from the number "2" mark as fast as you can for one minute. Write the number "3" where you stop.

5. Practice read Sections 1, 2 and 3 in one minute, and make your mark.

6. Read on from the number "3" as fast as you can for comprehension. Write the number "4" where you stop reading. Optional: Add to your Recall Pattern any new information obtained from any parts of the drill.

7. Go back to the number "2" as a starting point, and practice read through Section 4 in one minute.

8. Read on from number "4" as fast as you can for comprehension. Write the number "5" where you stop.

9. Go back to the number "3" as a starting point, and practice read through Section 5 in one minute.

10. Go back to the very beginning as a starting point, and practice read through Section 3 in one minute.

11. Go back to the beginning again, and this time practice read through Section 4, making your mark in one minute.

12. Go back to the beginning again, and practice read through all the sections in one minute. Make your mark!

13. Read in new material for good comprehension as fast as you can for one minute. Compute and record your rate, and add to your recall.

This is a weekly report of your progress at daily practice drills. With practice you will notice improvement in your reading rate from day to day and week to week. Make it your goal to attempt ever-increasing rates.

	Time spent on drill:	Range of reading rates:	Comments:
First Time	_____ mins.	_____ to _____ Low High	
Second Time	Time spent on drill: _____ mins.	Range of reading rates: _____ to _____ Low High	Comments:
Third Time	Time spent on drill: _____ mins.	Range of reading rates: _____ to _____ Low High	Comments:
Fourth Time	Time spent on drill: _____ mins.	Range of reading rates: _____ to _____ Low High	Comments:

Practice Summary

Record on your Progress Report Chart.

Total Time Spent on Drills: _____

Highest Reading Rate: _____

What You Need for This Lesson:

Evelyn Wood Course Guide

Audio CD #6

Pencil or pen

Blank paper

A book of your choice

Lesson 12

Evaluate Your Progress

**DO NOT READ THIS UNTIL
INSTRUCTED TO DO SO!**

The Boys' Life of Abraham Lincoln
by Helen Nicolay

The New President Lincoln and the War

The New President

After the nominations were made Douglas went on a tour of speech-making through the South. Lincoln, on the contrary, stayed quietly at home in Springfield. His personal habits and surroundings varied little during the whole of this campaign summer. Naturally he gave up active law practice, leaving his office in charge of his partner, William H. Herndon. He spent the time during the usual business hours of each day in the governor's room of the State-house at Springfield, attended only by his private secretary, Mr. Nicolay. Friends and strangers alike were able to visit him freely and without ceremony, and few went away without being impressed by the sincere frankness of his manner and conversation.   115

All sorts of people came to see him: those from far-away States, East and West, as well as those from nearer home. Politicians came to ask him for future favors, and many whose only motives were friendliness or curiosity called to express their good wishes and take the Republican candidate by the hand.

He wrote no public letters, and he made no speeches beyond a few words of thanks and greeting to passing street parades. Even the strictly private letters in which he gave his advice on points in the campaign were not more than a dozen in number;   214
but all through the long summer, while welcoming his throngs of visitors, listening to the tales of old settlers, making friends of strangers, and binding old friends closer by his ready sympathy, Mr. Lincoln watched political developments very closely, not merely to note the progress of his own chances, but with an anxious view to the future in case he should be elected. Beyond the ever-changing circle of friendly faces near him he saw the growing unrest and anger of the South, and doubtless felt the uncertainty of many good people in the North, who questioned the power of this untried Western man to guide the country through the coming perils.   325

Never over-confident of his own powers, his mind must at times have been full of misgivings; but it was only on the night of the election, November 6, 1860, when, sitting alone with the operators in the little telegraph-office at Springfield, he read the messages of Republican victory that fell from the wires until convinced of his election, that the overwhelming, almost crushing "weight of his coming duties and responsibilities fell upon him. In that hour, grappling resolutely and alone with the problem before him, he completed what was really the first act of his Presidency—the   422
choice of his cabinet, of the men who were to aid him. People who doubted the will or the wisdom of their Rail-splitter Candidate need have had no fear. A weak man would have chosen this little band of counselors—the Secretary of State, the Secretary of the Treasury, and the half-dozen others who were to stand closest to him and to be at the head of the great departments of the government—from among his personal friends. A man uncertain of his own power would have taken care that no other man of strong nature with a great following of his own should be there to dispute his authority.   532

Lincoln did the very opposite. He had a sincere belief in public opinion, and a deep respect for the popular will. In this case he felt that no men represented that popular will so truly as those whose names had been considered by the Republican National Convention in its choice of a candidate for President. So, instead of gathering about him his friends, he selected his most powerful rivals in the Republican party. William H. Seward, of New York, was to be his Secretary of State; Salmon P. Chase, of Ohio, his Secretary of the Treasury; Simon Cameron, of Pennsylvania, his Secretary of War; Edward Bates, of Missouri, his Attorney-General. The names of all of these men had been before the Convention. Each one had hoped to be President in his stead. For the other three members of his Cabinet he had to look elsewhere. Gideon Welles, of Connecticut, for Secretary of the Navy; Montgomery Blair, of Maryland, for Postmaster-General; and Caleb B. Smith, of Indiana, for Secretary of the Interior, were finally chosen. When people complained, as they sometimes did, that by this arrangement the cabinet consisted of four men who had been Democrats in the old days, and only three who had been Whigs, Lincoln smiled his wise, humorous smile and answered that he himself had been a Whig, and would always be there to make matters even. It is not likely that this exact list was in his mind on the night of the November election; but the principal names in it most certainly were. To some of these gentlemen he offered their appointments by letter. Others he asked to visit him in Springfield to talk the matter over. Much delay and some misunderstanding occurred before the list was finally completed: but when he sent it to the Senate, on the day after his inauguration, it was practically the one he had in his mind from the beginning.

650

744

854

***

Mr. Lincoln started on his journey to Washington on February 11, 1861 two days after Jefferson Davis had been elected President of the Confederate States of America. He went on a special train, accompanied by Mrs. Lincoln and their three children, his two private secretaries, and about a dozen personal friends. Mr. Seward had suggested that because of the unsettled condition of public affairs it would be better for the President-elect to come a week earlier; but Mr. Lincoln allowed himself only time comfortably to fill the engagements he had made to visit the State capitals and principal cities that lay on his way, to which he had been invited by State and town officials, regardless of party. The morning on which he left Springfield was dismal and stormy, but fully a thousand of his friends and neighbors assembled to bid him farewell. The weather seemed to add to the gloom and depression of their spirits, and the leave-taking was one of subdued anxiety, almost of solemnity. Mr. Lincoln took his stand in the waiting-room while his friends filed past him, often merely pressing his hand in silent emotion. The arrival of the rushing train broke in upon this ceremony, and the crowd closed about the car into which the President-elect and his party made their way. Just as they were starting, when the conductor had his hand upon the bell-rope, Mr. Lincoln stepped out upon the front platform and made the following brief and pathetic address. It was the last time his voice was to be heard in the city which had so long been his home:

968

1038

1122

"My Friends: No one not in my situation can appreciate my feeling of sadness at this parting. To this place and the kindness of these people I owe everything. Here I have lived a quarter of a century, and have passed from a young to an old man. Here my children have been born, and one is buried. I now leave, not knowing when or whether ever I may return, with a task before me greater than that which rested upon Washington. Without the assistance of that Divine Being who ever attended him, I

1216

---

cannot succeed. With that assistance I cannot fail. Trusting in Him who can go with me, and remain with you, and be everywhere for good, let us confidently hope that all will yet be well. To His care commending you, as I hope in your prayers you will commend me, I bid you an affectionate farewell."

1272

The conductor gave the signal, the train rolled slowly out of the station, and the journey to Washington was begun. It was a remarkable progress. At almost every station, even the smallest, crowds had gathered to catch a glimpse of the face of the President-elect, or at least to see the flying train. At the larger stopping-places these crowds swelled to thousands, and in the great cities to almost unmanageable throngs. Everywhere there were calls for Mr. Lincoln, and if he showed himself; for a speech. Whenever there was time, he would go to the rear platform of the car and bow as the train moved away, or utter a few words of thanks and greeting. At the capitals of Indiana, Ohio, New York, New Jersey, and Pennsylvania, and in the cities of Cincinnati, Cleveland, Buffalo, New York, and Philadelphia, halts of one or two days were made, the time being filled with formal visits and addresses to each house of the legislature, street processions, large evening receptions, and other ceremonies.

1376

1443

Party foes as well as party friends made up these expectant crowds. Every eye was eager, every ear strained, to get some hint of the thoughts and purposes of the man who was to be the guide and head of the nation in the crisis that every one now knew to be upon the country, but the course and end of which the wisest could not foresee. In spite of all the cheers and the enthusiasm, there was also an under-current of anxiety for his personal safety, for the South had openly boasted that Lincoln would never live to be inaugurated President. He himself paid no heed to such warnings; but the railroad officials, and others who were responsible for his journey, had detectives on watch at different points to report any suspicious happenings. Nothing occurred to change the program already agreed upon until the party reached Philadelphia; but there Mr. Lincoln was met by Frederick W. Seward, the son of his future Secretary of State, with an important message from his father. A plot had been discovered to do violence to, and perhaps kill, the President-elect as he passed through the city of Baltimore. Mr. Seward and General Scott, the venerable hero of the Mexican War, who was now at the head of the army, begged him to run no risk, but to alter his plans so that a portion of his party might pass through Baltimore by a night train without previous notice. The seriousness of the warning was doubled by the fact that Mr. Lincoln had just been told of a similar, if not exactly the same, danger, by a Chicago detective employed in Baltimore by one of the great railroad companies. Two such warnings, coming from entirely different sources, could not be disregarded; for however much Mr. Lincoln might dislike to change his plans for so shadowy a danger, his duty to the people who had elected him forbade his running any unnecessary risk. Accordingly, after fulfilling all his engagements in Philadelphia and Harrisburg on February 22, he and a single companion took a night train, passed quietly through Baltimore, and arrived in Washington about daylight on the morning of February 23. This action called forth much talk, ranging from the highest praise to ridicule and blame. A reckless newspaper reporter telegraphed all over the country the absurd story that he had traveled disguised in a Scotch cap and a long military cloak. There was, of course, not a word of truth in the absurd tale. The rest of the party followed Mr. Lincoln at the time originally planned. They saw great crowds in the streets of Baltimore, but there was now no occasion for violence.

1566

1696

1806

1893

In the week that passed between his arrival and the day of his inauguration Mr. Lincoln exchanged the customary visits of ceremony with President Buchanan, his cabinet, the Supreme Court, the two houses of Congress, and other dignitaries.

Careful preparations for the inauguration had been made under the personal direction of General Scott, who held the small military force in the city ready instantly to suppress any attempt to disturb the peace and quiet of the day.

1970

On the morning of the fourth of March President Buchanan and Citizen Lincoln, the outgoing and incoming heads of the government, rode side by side in a carriage from the Executive Mansion, or White House, as it is more commonly called, to the Capitol, escorted by an imposing procession; and at noon a great throng of people heard Mr. Lincoln read his inaugural address as he stood on the east portico of the Capitol, surrounded by all the high officials of the government. Senator Douglas, his unsuccessful rival, standing not an arm's length away from him, courteously held his hat during the ceremony. A cheer greeted him as he finished his address. Then the Chief Justice arose, the clerk opened his Bible, and Mr. Lincoln, laying his hand upon the book, pronounced the oath:

2104

"I, Abraham Lincoln, do solemnly swear that I will faithfully execute the office of President of the United States, and will, to the best of my ability, preserve, protect, and defend the Constitution of the United States."

Amid the thundering of cannon and the applause of all the spectators, President Lincoln and Citizen Buchanan again entered their carriage and drove back from the Capitol to the Executive Mansion, on the threshold of which Mr. Buchanan, warmly shaking the hand of his successor, expressed his wishes for the personal happiness of the new President, and for the national peace and prosperity.

2204

Lincoln and the War

Nothing more clearly shows the difference between President Lincoln and President Buchanan than the way in which the two men met the acts of the Southern Rebellion. President Buchanan temporized and delayed when he had plenty of power. President Lincoln, without a moment's hesitation accepted the great and unusual responsibility thrust upon him, and at once issued orders for buying ships, moving troops, advancing money to Committees of Safety, and for other military and naval measures for which at the moment he had no express authority from Congress. As soon as Congress came together on July 4, he sent a message explaining his action, saying: "It became necessary for me to choose whether, using only the existing means . . . . which Congress had provided, I should let the Government fall at once into ruin, or whether availing myself of the broader powers conferred by the Constitution in cases of insurrection, I would make an effort to save it with all its blessings for the present age and for posterity." Congress, it is needless to say, not only approved all that he had done, but gave him practically unlimited powers for dealing with the rebellion in future.

2299

2406

It soon became evident that no matter how ready and willing to fight for their country the 75,000 volunteers might be, they could not hope to put down the rebellion, because the time for which they had enlisted would be almost over before they could receive the training necessary to change them from valiant citizens into good soldiers. Another call was therefore issued, this time for men to serve three years or during the war, and also for a large number of sailors to man the new ships that the Government was straining every nerve to buy, build and otherwise make ready.

2508

More important, however, than soldiers trained or untrained, was the united will of the people of the North; and most important of all the steadfast and courageous soul of the man called to direct the struggle. Abraham Lincoln, the poor frontier boy, the struggling young lawyer, the Illinois politician, whom many, even among the Republicans who voted to elect him President, thought scarcely fit to hold a much smaller office, proved beyond question the man for the task gifted above all his associates with wisdom and strength to meet the great emergencies as they arose during the four years' war that had already begun.

2612

Since this is the story of Mr. Lincoln's life, and not of the Civil War, we cannot attempt to follow the history of the long contest as it unfolded itself day by day and month by month, or even to stop to recount a list of the great battles that drenched the land in blood. It was a mighty struggle, fought by men of the same race and kindred, often by brother against brother. Each fought for what he felt to be right; and their common inheritance of courage and iron will, of endurance and splendid bravery and stubborn pluck, made this battle of brothers the more bitter as it was the more prolonged. It ranged over an immense extent of country; but because Washington was the capital of the Union, and Richmond, Virginia, the capital of the Confederacy, and the desire of each side was to capture the chief city of the other, the principal fighting ground, during the whole war, lay between these two towns, with the Alleghany Mountains on the west, and Chesapeake Bay on the east. Between the Alleghenies and the Mississippi River another field of warfare developed itself, on which some of the hardest battles were fought, and the greatest victories won. Beyond the Mississippi again stretched another great field, bounded only by the Rocky Mountains and the Rio Grande. But the principal fighting in this field was near or even on the Mississippi, in the efforts made by both Unionists and Confederates to keep and hold the great highway of the river, so necessary for trade in time of peace, and for moving armies in time of war.

2736

2819

2886

On this immense battle-ground was fought one of the most costly wars of modern times, with soldiers numbering a million men on each side; in which, counting battles and skirmishes small and great, an average of two engagements a day were fought for four long years, two millions of money were used up every twenty-four hours, and during which the unholy prize of slavery, for which the Confederate States did battle, was completely swept away.

2961

Though the tide of battle ebbed and flowed, defeat and victory may be said to have been nearly evenly divided. Generally speaking, success was more often on the side of the South during the first half of the war; with the North, during the latter half. The armies were equally brave; the North had the greater territory from which to draw supplies; and the end came, not when one side had beaten the other, man for man, but when the South had been drained of fighting men and food and guns, and slavery had perished in the stress of war.

3061

Fortunately for all, nobody at the beginning dreamed of the length of the struggle. Even Lincoln's stout heart would have been dismayed if he could have foreseen all that lay before him. The task that he could see was hard and perplexing enough. Everything in Washington was in confusion. No President ever had such an increase of official work as Lincoln during the early months of his administration. The halls and ante-rooms of the Executive Mansion were literally crowded with people seeking appointment to office; and the new appointments that were absolutely necessary were not half finished when the firing on Fort Sumter began active war. This added to the difficulty of sifting the loyal from the disloyal, and the yet more pressing labor of organizing an immense new army.

3191

Hundreds of clerks employed in the Government Departments left their desks and hurried South, crippling the service just at the time when the sudden increase of work made their presence doubly needed. A large proportion of the officers of the Army and Navy, perhaps as many as one-third, gave their skill and services to the Confederacy, feeling that their allegiance was due to their State or section rather than to the general government. Prominent among these was Robert E. Lee, who had been made a colonel by Lincoln, and whom General Scott had recommended as the most promising officer to command the new force of 75,000 men called out by the President's proclamation. He chose instead to resign and cast his fortunes with the South, where he became the head of all the Confederate armies. The loss to the Union and gain to the Confederate cause by his action is hard to measure, since in him the Southern armies found a commander whose surpassing courage and skill inspired its soldiers long after all hope of success was gone. Cases such as this gave the President more anxiety than all else. It seemed impossible to know whom to trust. An officer might come to him in the morning protesting devotion to the Union, and by night be gone to the South. Mr. Lincoln used to say at this time that he felt like a man letting rooms at one end of his house while the other end was on fire.

3315

3440

The situation grew steadily worse. Maryland refused to allow United States soldiers to cross her territory, and the first attempt to bring troops through Baltimore from the North ended in a bloody riot, and the burning of railroad bridges to prevent help from reaching Washington. For three days Washington was entirely cut off from the North, either by telegraph or mail. General Scott hastily prepared the city for a siege, taking possession of all the large supplies of flour and provisions in town, and causing the Capitol and other public buildings to be barricaded. Though President Lincoln did not doubt the final arrival of help, he, like everyone else, was very anxious, and found it hard to understand the long delay. He knew that troops had started from the North. Why did they not arrive? They might not be able to go through Baltimore, but they could certainly go around it. The distance was not great. What if twenty miles of railroad had been destroyed, were the soldiers unable to march? Always calm and self-controlled, he gave no sign in the presence of others of the anxiety that weighed so heavily upon him. Very likely the visitors who saw him during those days thought that he hardly realized the plight of the city; yet an inmate of the White House, passing through the President's office when the day's work was done and he imagined himself alone, saw him pause in his absorbed walk up and down the floor, and gaze long out of the window in the direction from which the troops were expected to appear. Then, unconscious of any hearer, and as if the words were wrung from him by anguish, he exclaimed, "Why don't they come, why don't they come?"

3551

3656

3732

The New York Seventh Regiment was the first to "come." By a roundabout route it reached Washington on the morning of April 25, and, weary and travel-worn, but with banners flying and music playing, marched up Pennsylvania Avenue to the big white Executive Mansion, bringing cheer to the President and renewed courage to those timid citizens whose fright during this time had almost paralyzed the life of the town. Taking renewed courage they once more opened their houses and the shops that had been closed since the beginning of the blockade, and business began anew.

3627

The greater part of the three months' regiments had been ordered to Washington, and the outskirts of the capital soon became a busy military camp. The great Departments of the Government, especially of War and Navy, could not immediately handle the details of all this sudden increase of work. Men were volunteering rapidly enough, but there was sore need of rations to feed them, money to pay them, tents to

3897

shelter them, uniforms to clothe them, rifles to arm them, officers to drill them, and of transportation to carry them to the camps of instruction where they must receive their training and await further orders. In this carnival of patriotism and hurly-burly of organization the weaknesses as well as the virtues of human nature quickly showed themselves; and, as if the new President had not already enough to distress and harass his mind, almost every case of confusion and delay was brought to him for complaint and correction. On him also fell the delicate and serious task of deciding hundreds of novel questions as to what he and his cabinet ministers had and had not the right to do under the Constitution.

4019

The month of May slipped away in all these preparatory vexations; but the great machine of war, once started, moved on as it always does, from arming to massing of troops, and from that to skirmish and battle. In June small fights began to occur between the Union and Confederate armies. The first large battle of the war took place at Bull Run, about thirty-two miles southwest of Washington, on July 21, 1861. It ended in a victory for the Confederates, though their army was so badly crippled by. its losses that it made no further forward movement during the whole of the next autumn and winter. The shock of this defeat was deep and painful to the people of the North, not yet schooled to patience, or to the uncertainties of war. For weeks the newspapers, confident of success, had been clamoring for action, and the cry, "Forward to Richmond," had been heard on every hand. At first the people would not believe the story of a defeat; but it was only too true. By night the beaten Union troops were pouring into the fortifications around Washington, and the next day a horde of stragglers found their way across the bridges of the Potomac into the city.

4123

4226

President Lincoln received the news quietly, as was his habit, without any visible sign of distress or alarm, but he remained awake and in his office all that Sunday night, listening to the excited tales of congressmen and senators who, with undue curiosity, had followed the army and witnessed some of the sights and sounds of battle; and by dawn on Monday he had practically made up his mind as to the probable result and what he must do in consequence.

4307

The loss of the battle of Bull Run was a bitter disappointment to him. He saw that the North was not to have the easy victory it anticipated; and to him personally it brought a great and added care that never left him during the war. Up to that time the North had stood by him as one man in its eager resolve to put down the rebellion. From this time on, though quite as determined, there was division and disagreement among the people as to how this could best be done. Parties formed themselves for or against this or that general, or in favor of this or that method and no other of carrying on the war. In other words, the President and his "administration"—the cabinet and other officers under him—became, from this time on, the target of criticism for all the failures of the Union armies, and for all the accidents and mistakes and unforeseen delays of war. The self-control that Mr. Lincoln had learned in the hard school of his boyhood, and practiced during all the long struggle of his young manhood, had been severe and bitter training, but nothing else could have prepared him for the great disappointments and trials of the crowning years of his life. He had learned to endure patiently, to reason calmly, never to be unduly sure of his own opinion; but, having taken counsel of the best advice at his command, to continue in the path that he felt to be right, regardless of criticism or unjust abuse. He had daily and hourly to do all this. He was strong and courageous, with a steadfast belief that the right would triumph in the end; but his nature was at the same time sensitive and tender, and the sorrows and pain of others hurt him more than did his own.

4422

4510

4620

If you finish early...

If you finish reading the passage before the tone sounds, IMMEDIATELY BEGIN TIMING the amount of time left until the tone sounds. To compute your reading rate:

- Round off the amount of time you did not use to the nearest quarter minute. For example, 11 seconds would be 1/4 minute.

- Subtract the amount of time you did not use from three minutes to find the amount of time you did use.

- Divide the total number of words (4,620) by the amount of time you used.

1. **Which statement best describes Lincoln's strategy during the campaign? (325 words)**
   a. He kept a very low profile with few speeches or letters.
   b. He planned a train trip across the Midwest so he could stay in touch with the people.
   c. He held intense strategy meetings twice a week.
   d. He had regular briefings about Douglas' activities and poll rankings.

2. **How did Lincoln hear that he won the election? (398 words)**
   a. His campaign advisor arrived on horseback with the news.
   b. He was in the Capitol building where the State Senate announced it.
   c. He was sitting with the telegraph operators in Springfield.
   d. His wife woke him to tell him the news.

3. **How did Lincoln select his cabinet? (605 words)**
   a. He chose powerful men who had been his rivals to get a cross section of opinions.
   b. He chose his most trusted friends and advisors since he knew he could count on them.
   c. He chose the people who supported his candidacy, as a way of thanking them for their support.
   d. He chose a cross-section of people who would support his initiatives and carry them out.

4. **What was the mood in Lincoln's home town when he left for Washington? (1122 words)**
   a. Loud and celebratory
   b. Solemn and gloomy
   c. Quietly excited
   d. Lincoln left secretly so there wouldn't be any fanfare.

5. **Why did the railroad have detectives on the journey to Washington? (1577 words)**
   a. Because the South said Lincoln would never live to be inaugurated.
   b. Many of the frontier towns they would go through were lawless.
   c. They needed to interview the Lincoln's about the recent death of their son.
   d. Security checks needed to be completed on their family and closest friends.

6. **Which President did Lincoln replace? (1970 words)**
   a. Andrew Johnson
   b. Franklin Pierce
   c. Zachary Taylor
   d. James Buchanan

7. **What did Lincoln do when he took office – before having Congress' approval? (2296 words)**
   a. Put his cabinet in place and started holding meetings
   b. Signed the Emancipation Proclamation
   c. Began moving money, equipment, and troops in anticipation of war
   d. Declared war on the South

8. **Where were the majority of the Civil War battles held? (2886 words)**
   a. West of the Allegheny mountains
   b. Between the Union and Confederate capitals
   c. Around Fort Sumter
   d. Along the banks of the Delaware river

9. **Why was Washington cut off from the North at the beginning of the war? (3501 words)**
   a. The South had attacked the telegraph and mail outposts.
   b. Maryland would not allow soldiers to cross her territory.
   c. The railroads had been destroyed.
   d. A self-imposed communication blackout was instituted until they could determine which government workers were for the North versus the South.

10. **According to the passage, why was the Battle of Bull Run significant? (4226 words)**
    a. It helped Lincoln to determine which officers would make the best commanders.
    b. It prevented the Northern troops from making it down to Washington for fortification.
    c. The defeat showed the North that the war wouldn't be an easy victory.
    d. It was a proving ground for new tactics and weapons.

Number of Questions Responsible for Answering

	1	2	3	4	5	6	7	8	9	10
1	100	50	33	25	20	16	14	13	11	10
2		100	67	50	40	33	29	25	22	20
3			100	75	60	50	43	38	33	30
4				100	80	67	57	50	44	40
5					100	83	72	63	56	50
6						100	86	75	67	60
7							100	88	78	70
8								100	89	80
9									100	90
10										100

Number of Questions Correct

Write everything you remember from the selection you have read. Do NOT look back at the reading. Write only one item on each line.

More Important Points	Details & Supporting Points

Go on to the next page if you need more room.

More Important Points	Details & Supporting Points

Total number of Important Points: _____

Total number of Supporting Points: _____

Could you have written more with more time? _____

Average words per minute reading rate: _____

Appendix

Lesson 1: Pre-Assessment Test

1. C
2. A
3. B
4. C
5. C
6. D
7. B
8. A
9. D
10. D

Lesson 12: Post-Assessment Test

1. A
2. C
3. A
4. B
5. A
6. D
7. C
8. B
9. B
10. C

Progress Report Chart

for _____

Lesson One:

Beginning Rate: _____WPM

Comprehension Score:_____

Number of items recalled:

Major: _____ Minor: _____

Total: _____

Lesson Two:

W-A-T-E-R Rate: _____

Extension Drill Rate: _____

Ending Reading Rate: _____

Supplementary Practice

# of Extension Drills: _____

Highest Reading Rate: _____

Lesson Three:

Opening Reading Rate: _____

Push-Down Drill Rate: _____

Ending Reading Rate: _____

Supplementary Practice

# of Push-Down Drills: _____

Highest Reading Rate: _____

Lesson Four:

Opening Reading Rate: _____

Add Half a Page Drill : _____

Supplementary Practice

# of Add Half a Page Drills: _____

Highest Reading Rate: _____

Lesson Five:

Push-Up Drill Start: _____

Push-Up Drill Finish: _____

Supplementary Practice

# of Push-Up Drills: _____

Highest Reading Rate: _____

Lesson Six:

Ending Reading Rate: _____

Number of items recalled:

Major : _____ Minor: _____

Total: _____

Supplementary Practice

# of pages in 10 minutes

Day 1: _____ Day 2: _____

Day 3: _____ Day 4: _____

# of Push Up Drills: _____

Highest Reading Rate: _____

Lesson Seven:

Opening Reading Rate: _____

Ending Reading Rate: _____

Supplementary Practice

# of Dynamic Drills : _____

Highest Reading Rate: _____

Lesson Eight:

Power Drill Rate: _____

Supplementary Practice

# of Dynamic Drills: _____

Highest Reading Rate: _____

Lesson Nine:

Opening Reading Rate: _____

Supplementary Practice

# of Study/Depth Drills: _____

Highest Reading Rate: _____

# of Push-Down Drills: _____

Highest Reading Rate: _____

Lesson Ten:

Opening Reading Rate: _____

On-Screen 'Old' Rate: _____

On-Screen 'Pace' Rate: _____

Supplementary Practice

# of pages in 15 minutes

Day 1: _____   Day 2: _____

Day 3: _____   Day 4: _____

# of Add Half a Page Drills

Highest Reading Rate: _____

Lesson Eleven:

Overlap Drill Rate: _____

Supplementary Practice

# of Overlap Drills: _____

Optional review of Drills:

3. _____   4: _____

5: _____   7: _____

Lesson Twelve:

Opening Reading Rate: _____

Combination Drill Rate: _____

Final Reading Rate: _____

Comprehension Score: _____

Number of items recalled

Major: _____   **Minor:** _____

Total: _____

Lesson One:

Beginning Rate: _____WPM

Comprehension Score:_____

Number of items recalled:

Major: _____ Minor: _____

Total: _____

Lesson Two:

W-A-T-E-R Rate: _____

Extension Drill Rate: _____

Ending Reading Rate: _____

Supplementary Practice

# of Extension Drills: _____

Highest Reading Rate: _____

Lesson Three:

Opening Reading Rate: _____

Push-Down Drill Rate: _____

Ending Reading Rate: _____

Supplementary Practice

# of Push-Down Drills: _____

Highest Reading Rate: _____

Lesson Four:

Opening Reading Rate: _____

Add Half a Page Drill : _____

Supplementary Practice

# of Add Half a Page Drills: _____

Highest Reading Rate: _____

Lesson Five:

Push-Up Drill Start: _____

Push-Up Drill Finish: _____

Supplementary Practice

# of Push-Up Drills: _____

Highest Reading Rate: _____

Lesson Six:

Ending Reading Rate: _____

Number of items recalled:

Major : _____ Minor: _____

Total: _____

Supplementary Practice

# of pages in 10 minutes

Day 1: _____ Day 2: _____

Day 3: _____ Day 4: _____

# of Push Up Drills: _____

Highest Reading Rate: _____

Lesson Seven:

Opening Reading Rate: _____

Ending Reading Rate: _____

Supplementary Practice

# of Dynamic Drills : _____

Highest Reading Rate: _____

Lesson Eight:

Power Drill Rate: _____

Supplementary Practice

# of Dynamic Drills: _____

Highest Reading Rate: _____

Lesson Nine:

Opening Reading Rate: _____

Supplementary Practice

# of Study/Depth Drills: _____

Highest Reading Rate: _____

# of Push-Down Drills: _____

Highest Reading Rate: _____

Lesson Ten:

Opening Reading Rate: _____

On-Screen 'Old' Rate: _____

On-Screen 'Pace' Rate: _____

Supplementary Practice

# of pages in 15 minutes

Day 1: _____   Day 2: _____

Day 3: _____   Day 4: _____

# of Add Half a Page Drills

Highest Reading Rate: _____

Lesson Eleven:

Overlap Drill Rate: _____

Supplementary Practice

# of Overlap Drills: _____

Optional review of Drills:

3. _____   4: _____

5: _____   7: _____

Lesson Twelve:

Opening Reading Rate: _____

Combination Drill Rate: _____

Final Reading Rate: _____

Comprehension Score: _____

Number of items recalled

Major: _____   **Minor:** _____

Total: _____